5 PILLARS

of

love for self, life & others

Bernadette Laxamana

BSc, MBA

BERNADETTE LAXAMANA
The 5 Pillars of Love: for Self, Life & Others

Copyright © 2019 by Bernadette Laxamana
First edition

ISBN
978-1-9990477-0-2 (Print)
978-1-9990477-1-9 (E-Book)

BOOK DESIGN Jazmin Welch
EDITOR Kelsey Straight
PUBLISHING SUPPORT The Self Publishing Agency

The author of this book does not dispense medical advice or prescribe the use of any technique as a form of treatment for physical, emotional, or medical problems without the advice of a physician, either directly or indirectly. The intent of the author is only to offer information of a general nature to help you in your quest for emotional, physical, and spiritual well-being. In the event you use any of the information in this book for yourself, the author and the publisher assume no responsibility for your actions.

*Dedicated to the Lord my God, my Higher Self,
and all those desiring to experience deep inner peace
through the practice of love.*

85 Part Three: Life

PREFACE

"It is hard to love others as you love yourself, if you don't love yourself."
—DALAI LAMA

Love! In itself such an expressive word, and yet it's probably the most misunderstood. I wanted to write a book on a subject that I wish to master. It's difficult for me to love myself unconditionally everyday and far too easy to succumb to rejection and negative self-judgment. I desire to embrace self-love as my natural state, no matter what's going on around me—**I want a love that endures and lasts**.

In *The Book of Joy: Lasting Happiness in a Changing World*, the Dalai Lama expresses shock at hearing how we wrestle with self-hatred: "We spend so much of our lives climbing a pyramid of achievement, where we're constantly being evaluated and judged—and often found to be not making the grade." It's so easy to live a life defined by fulfillment in material things, rather than satisfaction in joyful experiences—a life that stems from loving oneself wholeheartedly and transferring that love to others.

I seek the kind of self-love described in **1 Corinthians 13: 4-8**: "Love is patient; love is kind. It does not envy; it does not boast, it is not proud. It does not dishonor others; it is not self-seeking, it is not easily angered, it keeps no record of wrongs. Love does not delight in evil but rejoices with the truth. It always protects, always trusts, always hopes, always perseveres. Love never fails."

This is the love I seek from God: for myself, my loved ones, and my community. I believe the foundation of love lies in what I call **The 5 Pillars**: Acceptance, Appreciation, Desire, Light-heartedness, and Freedom to fully express oneself. As I practice each pillar, I love more and more of myself, leading to a divine transformation: the more I nurture my self-love, the more it flows effortlessly and elegantly towards other people and parts of my life. To all of you who read this book, may it be a channel for personal peace.

Self

PART ONE

INTRODUCTION

Congratulations for taking this bold and powerful step towards transforming your life. You're one step closer to a whole new identity, full of love for yourself, the people around you, and the world at large. Life is about more than feeling overwhelmed by others' troubles and opinions, more than the perpetual state of wanting more and more material *things*. When you settle into the wrong mentality, you only come up with empty actions and poor results. When you have a shaky framework, it becomes so hard to love yourself, your life, and the people around you. To redefine the nature of these forces—attaining fulfillment and true meaning— you must adopt the right mindset and take the necessary steps.

These pillars guide you towards a fulfilled life, but you should be prepared: it does not involve a simple "on/off" switch. There's a lot of work to be done, but afterwards you'll marvel at the beauty existing inside you. The world will watch as you blossom, providing the energy to attain the heights of your desires. Apply these principles in your life, career, and everyday encounters. Follow the roadmap of this book, get intimate with your beliefs about love, and watch your life change for the better. These pillars provide a model for developing a life-changing skill-set. By the end of this book, you'll have discovered valuable strategies for attaining greater satisfaction and life success.

ACCEPTANCE **1**

The First Pillar of Love is Self-Acceptance.

Self-acceptance is the willingness to give yourself unconditional love, without taking note of your flaws. It means loving, nurturing, and letting yourself blossom into something more. According to Merriam-Webster's Dictionary, "to accept" means "to receive willingly or to give approval to." True acceptance, therefore, is the willingness for something or someone to belong to you.

Take the example of a child accepting a teddy bear. When a child receives the gift of a teddy bear, she doesn't merely hug its arm, or a leg, she clutches the bear wholeheartedly. She embraces all of it as something that belongs to her. True acceptance can also be ascribed to that connection between a mother and her newborn child. When a child is born, the mother accepts her newfound love with a whole heart. She doesn't look at the eyes and wish they were somehow different; she doesn't look at the nose and wish for it to change. She sees her baby with wonder, beauty, and excitement.

What's strange about this is how that same mother may never accept herself with comparable unconditional love. **Wouldn't it be excellent if we all beheld ourselves with the same wonder, beauty, and excitement as we do our children?** A baby sleeps, cries, poops, pees, flails her hands, and kicks her feet, and still the mother claps with joy. The desire to change the baby is seldom felt by mothers; the baby's actions, sounds, and feelings are fully embraced—in a word, the child is *accepted*.

Let's talk about the body. Fundamentally, my body belongs to me, and yours belongs to you, but sometimes society thinks our bodies should be different. When our bodies fall short of the societal criteria, we often turn away from ourselves and surrender to the norm. However, upon rejecting the norm, we might adopt behaviors that vindicate our sense of rebellion. In the book *Willpower*, Roy Baumeister and John Tierney call this syndrome the **What the Hell Effect**. For example:

Oh, I might as well keep eating this and that... what's the use of starving myself!

I don't like what I am, so I'll keep eating and drinking what I want, when I want it. Might as well not exercise either... what's the point?

I don't want to face it, so I'll just watch TV or spend time on social media.

Why can't my abs be like hers? Why don't I look that good in heels? Red looks better on her than I could ever dream of for myself! She sure has it all, and what do I get? Nothing!

It's interesting how we worship the bodies of others, big shot celebrities or photo-shopped figures in the media, when the bodies we have provide so much for us. We take our bodies everywhere we go; they are the vessels that guide us through our lives. The first commandment from God applies here: "**Thou shall not have other Gods before me.**" I believe the Divine in us—or as some would call it, our *higher spirit*—prefers that we embrace and accept our bodies, those we have now, opposed to chasing some ideal version of ourselves that does not exist and cannot give us life.

When we worship the bodies of others, we choose their nature over our own, fundamentally rejecting ourselves—and what happens when we refuse something? We turn away and forget about it. Therefore, we cannot impact, contribute, or make a difference with respect to something we've refused. Instead, what if we made the choice to claim our bodies? What happens when we truly own something? In a few words, we take care of and cherish that something, eventually using it to transform our lives. To impact the forces of our lives, we must first own them entirely, because accepting is the act of possessing.

So what actions can we take to accept ourselves? Let's start with our bodies. What steps can we take to recognize and accept our bodies today, instead of waiting to feel thinner, stronger, healthier, leaner, sexier, etc. Virginia Satir once said, "We need four hugs a day for survival. We need eight hugs a day for maintenance. We need 12 hugs a day for growth."

I like being hugged, and I give hugs. Think of a time when you were warmly embraced. How did you feel in that moment, and can you intensify that feeling, making it stronger and more profound? Focus on the feeling while keeping your arms wrapped around yourself. Repeat the following mantra **12** times, remembering that the more you repeat it, the more intense and accurate it becomes: **This is my body; I choose it, I own it**.

When you say, *I choose my body*, you're actually choosing yourself over all other bodies, thereby claiming ownership of who you are. Whatever else exists out there is simply not yours; you have something different and insatiably unique. Your inner voice may protest: *I don't want my body; I want her body*. Listen to that voice critically—can you really own another person's body? Is it even possible to own someone else's face, breasts, hips, butt, or thighs? This is life, not plastic surgery.

You might adore another woman's body as one adores a piece of art, but what you really admire is the product of her spirit. Instead you must learn to love yourself—wholeheartedly, unabashedly— and this begins with giving yourself hugs. By hugging ourselves, we perform an act of love and acceptance, embracing who we are. Keep initiating the action and the emotions will follow. Every time you hear that pesky, critical voice, your first response should be to hug yourself.

When a child is bullied, do adults yell at the child some more? No, we hug the child and find ways to care for them. Sometimes the same thing happens in our own minds—upon noticing the "bullying" in our heads, we must stop that action and simultaneously give ourselves a heartfelt hug. Of the billions of bodies in the world, we picked the one we own; we chose ourselves with loving acceptance. What about our brains? Our minds themselves? They've helped us get this far, but sometimes we worship other people's minds above our own. While the minds of others may appear to be endowed with more beauty and brilliance, remember that they have their challenges too.

Take a moment to embrace your mind: **This is my mind; I choose it, I own it**. If you say this enough, other people will cease to have power over your life. Give your mind the validation and energy it needs to expand. When we give notice to smarter people, the mind contracts, filling with misgivings and apparent shortcomings—but when we see the unique brilliance of our brains, the mind immediately expands.

What about actions? When you don't feel kind enough, generous enough, patient enough, or noticeably humble, when you're too strict, loud, proud, or rigid, do you falter in your steps? Do you allow your inner voice to take over with negative self-talk? In judging ourselves negatively, we reject who we are in favor of some moral code, belief, or expectation that ultimately belongs to someone else. From there, we begin to wither on the inside. When something is labelled with an adverse outcome, because somebody cried, got hurt, or was generally offended, we immediately proceed with self-rejection. We turn away from ourselves. What works better in that moment is to embrace ourselves and say: **This is my decision, my voice, and my experience. I choose and own all of me**.

For every wrong action we take—in every moment of adverse judgment or shaky feelings of not being *enough*—we do two things. First, we forget our intentions for acceptance, and second, we provide false endings for the stories playing out in our minds. Let's take a typical example: gossip, or any conversation where people share judgments and details before verifying the facts. Now, let's say your gossip-sesh is discovered by the person you were talking about—naturally, one would expect some negative fallout.

Now let's say you take that fallout personally, beating yourself up or playing the victim. At this point, you've forgotten the original intention behind your actions (the choice to gossip), thereby creating a new narrative chain-of-events. This narrative differs significantly from the truth, serving only to validate your sense of victimhood. However, there is a positive or noble intent behind most actions. In choosing to gossip, perhaps you wanted to incite connection and camaraderie with another human being. Perhaps you were telling an inspiring story, offering words of encouragement, or simply talking about your feelings.

In a different scenario, your child returns home in a bad mood. You decide to inquire, but she won't share her feelings, so instead you keep prodding until things escalate and somehow the situation deteriorates into a yelling fight. In such a scenario, your next move might be to send that child to her room, but it doesn't end there. When your husband comes home, overlapping emotions continue to cloud your judgment, and you label yourself and the event negatively. *You shouldn't have said x…you shouldn't have done x…you should have said y…you shouldn't have done y…you were wrong…she was wrong…you were terrible…she was bad…and onwards and etcetera forever.*

If you step back and remember the true intentions behind your actions (the asking and prodding, the raising of your voice, and finally the escalation), you might discover they were noble. The asking and prodding was carried out in hopes of making a difference. You were trying to help and inspire connection, showing immense love for your daughter and empowering her to do the same. What you wanted to achieve was unmistakably positive, beautiful, and noble. This kind of thinking is applicable to every occasion. If you take a moment to examine the instant before the action—that split second before you leapt into the unknown, you'll notice the nobility of your intentions.

In order to remove yourself from the spiral of blame, rejection, and adverse judgment, find solace in knowing that whatever happened arose from noble intentions. Shift your attention away from the action and remember your purpose. Make no mistake, this is not the end: the same action that evoked the 'blame game' may morph, transform, and evolve into something more in the future. There are millions of possibilities; for example, your "gossip-sesh" might actually inspire the other person to change, or it could create space between you and the herd, thus making room for new realms of friendship and connection. No matter what potentially adverse outcomes might dance in your head, they are not real—they are merely fantasies. By jumping to conclusions, labeling, or judging yourself poorly, you bookend the drama. Instead of applying positivity and open-mindedness, you abandon the moment before a solution can be found.

For every action, there's a positive or noble intention, and every action comes armed with an ever evolving conclusion. That conclusion continues indefinitely, as long as you're alive, it can morph, evolve, transform, and expand into something new. When you start jumping to conclusions, you stop the honest flow of peace and possibility, but your intentions still stream from that original action, so **let go and watch things evolve naturally**.

When you accept that many actions have honorable intentions, you feel a noble essence within you, and this would not be possible if nobility wasn't part of who you are. To use an analogy, if you smell a strong cup of coffee, there's almost certainly actual coffee somewhere nearby; our inner worlds work much the same. As human beings, the negative judgments we make about our actions stem from worrying that we're not enough. This can take many forms, for example:

I yelled at my kid; I'm not a good mother.
I didn't speak up; I'm not a good communicator.
I didn't get the job; I'll never be smart enough.
I am broken.
I am weak.
I don't have enough discipline.

I am not this; I am not that; I didn't do this; I didn't do that: I don't have this; I forgot that—and onwards and etcetera, until the thinking turns to madness.

We desire things beyond our reach, but the true treasures are buried within our bodies. The only gifts we need are here beneath our ribcages—all we have to do is remember who we are. When we reflect on conflicted actions, we look for what went wrong, producing thoughts like, *I did that and it's my fault; I am not enough of x*. But if we go back to our intentions, hearing our purpose sound from within, we remember the essence of our feelings.

Returning to the gossip analogy, let's say your true intentions were sharing and connection, desires present inside us all. If connection and sharing come from a place of love, then love must be present and accounted for inside you. Your mind simply took action to express it. We spiral into negativity when we allow others' actions, behaviors, or opinions to define the reality of our essence. Of course, it's important to be aware of the moments when you raised your voice, said something hurtful, or procrastinated about work, but how you interpret and take responsibility for these actions is much more critical.

You can beat yourself up about it, furthering your pain and disempowerment while rejecting the consequences of your actions—or you can accept what happened. If you did what you did with pure intentions, learn from that experience and try nurturing deeper feelings of peace and love in the future. Otherwise, you can expect to take the same negative action again and again. **It's all a matter of choice, so what do you choose?**

The results stay the same, so decide upon your intentions and take the next best action! True acceptance means embracing the notion that whoever you are right now—wherever you are, whatever you are doing—points to who you'll become. **The present**

can only be called a blessing, so you are blessed. What you have and don't have, whoever you are being and not being—everyone and everything here right now—is a gift and blessing to you. To not accept this is to reject yourself. To deny the glory in what you have right now is the same as pretending you're somewhere else. There is no peace or joy in such actions. There's simply no way to enjoy the moment. By not accepting the reality of your life, you fail to create space to love yourself with all your heart. Without acceptance, we never fully learn to love.

ACTION STEPS!

STEP 1   Study yourself in the mirror, beginning from your eyes, and notice how they gleam. Now say to yourself: *I commit to accept all of myself, including the past that led me here. Who I am now is the best version of me at present.* Keep saying these words and watch as you change your self-perceptions.

STEP 2   Now get a journal and objectively recount any past personal events that were negative in nature. It's important that you do this without playing the blame game. Look at what you've written and accept it as reality. What happened belongs to the past; it should no longer hurt you. Say to yourself, *I will always seek to vest nobility in my actions.* For as long as nobility lives inside you, there will always be noble intentions behind your thoughts, perceptions, and behaviors, so learn to embrace this reality, instead of lapsing into self-abuse.

STEP 3   Looking at these events, can you see how negative emotions made things worse? It's time to stop predicting negative outcomes and results. It's time to let go of the toxic self-talk and simply take a deep breath, letting the negative energy flow away from your body. Say to yourself, *I will stop myself when I make negative predictions or judgments.* When we fail to accomplish this, our imagination controls our perceptions, creating a slew of false endings in turn. William Shakespeare once wrote, "there is nothing either good or bad, but thinking makes it so."

STEP 4 Write about the parts of your body that you don't appreciate. Look at them and consider the good things they've brought to you. If you step away from the negative energy, you'll accept them as part of your gene makeup. Society did not create you and it should not make determinations about your body. From now on, resist being swayed by the thoughts of others; learn to accept yourself for you.

The Story of the the Beautiful Mare and Sei Weng

"A man named Sei Weng owned a beautiful mare. The horse was praised far and wide, until one day, this beautiful horse disappeared. The villagers offered sympathy to Sei Weng for his great misfortune, but he merely said, 'That's the way it is.'

A few days later, the lost mare returned, followed by a beautiful wild stallion. The village congratulated Sei Weng for his good fortune. He said, 'That's the way it is.'

Sometime later, Sei Weng's only son, while riding the stallion, fell off and broke his leg. The village people once again expressed their sympathies for Sei Weng's misfortune. Sei Weng again said, 'That's the way it is.'

Soon after that, war broke out, and all the young men of the village were drafted and killed in battle—except Sei Weng's lame son. The village people were amazed at Sei Weng's good luck. His son was the only young man alive in the village, but Sei Weng kept the same attitude. Despite all the turmoil, gains, and losses, he gave the same reply, 'That's the way it is.'"

—*"The Parable of the Taoist Farmer"* (BRIANTAYLOR.COM)

APPRECIATION **2**

The Second Pillar of Love is Self-Appreciation.

Merriam Webster's Dictionary defines appreciation as "to value, admire highly, or otherwise increase the value of." When you value something highly and fully, you're inclined to enhance the value of it. When you value money, you hope that it appreciates in value; however, when you hear that another person has money, does it change your own bank account positively or negatively? Is their money your money? No, in reality, its value does not belong to you. The same is true with our bodies, minds, actions, and lives. Unless we choose and own ourselves, we cannot activate enough self-worth to positively appreciate our values. We cannot create value from something we don't own, and we cannot appreciate things we don't value. In other words, whatever you choose to appreciate will inevitably appreciate in worth.

This process of positive appreciation is not easy. Our minds are programmed to focus on negatives. According to a study by Cleveland Clinic, the average person has 60,000 thoughts per day: 95% of them repeat each day, and a stunning 80% of them are *negative* (Discover Magazine). It's easier to focus on whatever isn't working, but whatever you're criticizing, rejecting, or condemning only creates negative energy in the corresponding parts of yourself.

Whenever you focus on being impatient, you increase the value of that impatience, which means you negatively appreciate your impatience. Whenever you focus on being undisciplined or lazy, you fuel that reality and increase its value, while negatively appreciating your laziness. Energy only flows in the direction of attention, so it's imperative to focus on positive actions and values. To change this mental programming of negative appreciation, we must learn to appreciate our bodies, minds, and everyday lives.

For our bodies, we've already established that we must choose and own them, but what do we value about our bodies? A typical answer might conform to the dictates of society, but know that in placing higher value on society's perspectives than on your own, you're only limiting your potential. For instance, our society places value on being thin. A desire for thinness is the norm, but nonetheless, we all possess higher values than those derived from being *'thin.'* **If you value being thin, it should not be because of society, but because of you.** Ask yourself the question: *What value do I place on my body—what is important to me?*

When it comes to my body, I value strength, excellence, and self-care. My definition of these attributes might differ from yours, and that's okay. I expect your values to be yours. The important thing is learning to value what makes you unique and taking action to increase those forces inside you. Since I value strength, I choose to work-out daily and vary the nature of my workouts, thereby increasing or "appreciating" the value of strength. As I appreciate my strength, I appreciate my body. I also value excellence, so I choose to nourish my body with excellent food; as I increase my physical caliber, I appreciate my body more. When it comes to self-care, I nonetheless choose to indulge once in a while, eating my favorite foods or having weekly massages, in turn appreciating my body even further.

What about the mind? In the previous chapter, we discussed the dangers of telling yourself that other people are better than you. Again, choose to value your own mind. I value mastery, learning, and growth, all inherently broad subjects, but I can address them together by amassing my knowledge in a book. To increase my appreciation of mastery, I could write every day, making a habit of putting words on paper—as I appreciate my mastery of book-writing, I appreciate the value of my mind. I also value learning, which I appreciate by reading books, listening to the radio, or playing a new instrument. As I appreciate my learning, the appreciation for my mind grows deeper. Finally, I can appreciate the value of growth by taking action in areas that scare me; as I appreciate my growth, I again foster appreciation for my mind.

What about your relationships, achievements, and possessions? Sometimes, we can determine value without comparing ourselves to others. When we compare ourselves to others, we immediately forget to accept and appreciate who we are. It works better to accept our own relationships, achievements, and possessions: *They are mine; I choose them, I own them.* Once we take ownership, we begin to instill value and appreciation. Appreciating others will be discussed later on in this book, but for now, let's talk about you.

ACTION STEPS!

STEP 1   Find a journal and write about the areas of your life that need more appreciation! Some areas might include health, self-care, personal development, spirituality, compassion, leadership, or mindset, but these are only examples. Instead, use these headings to brainstorm, writing a full description of similar things that you wish to appreciate underneath each one.

STEP 2   Now, using a different sheet, write down everything that you value most about your body. Do not judge your perspectives; simply give yourself space to value. There are no right or wrong values. Over time, you'll learn to value more aspects of yourself, kick-starting multiple transformation processes, but it's all about your little list for now. Focus on what values are important at present. You can add, subtract, or change the order anytime.

STEP 3   Write down the steps you'll take towards appreciating yourself. Remember to be very specific in your list. Slowly, you'll notice improvement in different areas of your life. Try as much as possible to take baby steps, not revolutionary leaps. Bigger steps require more energy to build and sustain that momentum, often leading to burnout, fatigue, procrastination, or worse—you might even quit before kick-starting your goals. Take things one step at a time. It's also important that these steps are taken within a specific and brief time frame, allowing you to monitor your progress.

STEP 4   Review this list daily, adding at least three more things that you appreciate about yourself. As you start appreciating your values through deliberate actions, you change your entire programming, as if reformatting yourself for positive instead of negative appreciation.

At this point, it's clear how working to increase appreciation activates the Law of Attraction. This basically means you are a human magnet. You attract people, events, or experiences that are congruent with your dominant thoughts. As you look around at the world, taking action to appreciate what you value, you unconsciously attract more of the same. This keeps your mind on what you want, instead of what you don't need. Your thoughts—those tiny perceptions that loop through your mind—become self-fulfilling prophecies and show up everywhere in your life. When you focus your mind on self-acceptance and appreciation, you turn into a loving version of yourself. In the words of Earl Nightingale, **"You become what you think about."**

3

The Third Pillar of Love is Desire.

Once we accept and fully appreciate ourselves, we are ready for the third pillar of self-love, the ability to pair desire with detachment. The Oxford English Dictionary defines "desire" as a "strong" feeling of "wanting to have something or wishing for something to happen."

I've always had huge goals for my business; I strove to hit seven figures in revenue within the first few years, but with my team's work and God's blessings, we managed to exceed that number.

Now my goal is to double it. My desire for financial success is also a desire to grow: doubling my revenue requires mastering more areas of my business, (sales, marketing, coaching, tech, etc). I also have to grow in grace, leadership, excellence, and care; in other words, my dream of making millions is also a dream of making a difference in millions of people's lives.

One night, I was praying and meditating, agitated by concerns that I desired something "wrong." I felt guilty that perhaps I didn't know how to be grateful for what I have. After all, why should I want more? In the process of achieving my desires, I'd already made a positive difference in thousands of people's lives—my clients, my family, my team, and my team's families. My clients were more prosperous, enjoying greater peace of mind from using our services. For my team members and their families, it was the same story: in working with me, they achieved greater peace of mind, owing to increased financial security and the knowledge that their work mattered.

From an early age, I've always been goal-oriented. I set targets and work to hit them by specific dates. My parents often suggest that I slow down, arguing that I can still be ambitious and content without driving myself crazy. One day, I decided to try out their definition of happiness by being okay with what I had, instead of reaching for more. I didn't take extra initiative at work, nor did I seek to realize bigger goals. Within the next four weeks, my sales numbers dropped. Not only did my excellence lessen at work, I noticed the same habits creeping into other areas of my life. I realize now that being content does not mean changing my habits to fit someone else's expectations. As I push for higher desires, I show up for myself more, igniting a greater desire to transform my life. I'm reaching forwards with tremendous passion, and my jet-stream of energy leaves corresponding patterns across the skies of my life.

When I have a big desire or goal, I become unreasonable to most people. I say "unreasonable" because while other people view my priorities as illogical or misplaced, to me they make perfect sense. The values and needs that underlie my desires are actually quite unique. I've also noticed that when I move towards what I desire, everything around me transforms, as if compelled by the force of movement and Newton's First Law.

After decades of learning, reading, training, and coaching, I know it's important that my desires and goals are driven by my higher purpose, but equally important is remaining detached from the *meaning* of certain results. There are plenty of books about our higher purpose, with countless exercises to help one articulate that purpose for themselves. The universal truth is that all human beings want to experience happiness, joy, and peace. That said, we do not follow the same paths to achieve these things, because we are all unique and different.

For me, my purpose these days is to create a positive, lasting difference for millions of people. I have a passion for expanding the nobility in everyone. As discussed in the last chapter, every action has a noble intention, which I seek to transfer to those around me. This becomes the foundation for all my desires—big and small. I love myself, so I give free rein to all my desires. I desire what I desire; I love what I love. With this foundation, I love what I do and do what I love.

ACTION STEPS!

STEP 1 What is your **purpose** in life? Take time to assess and decide before writing it down. Sometimes we think our purpose is written down in books; however, while books help to direct us towards our purpose, be careful not to define yourself by another person's dreams or aspirations.

Instead, try using meditation to find your purpose. With meditation, you connect with your inner self, encouraging energy and clarity in turn. Even if your purpose at the moment seems relatively small, you must trust that it will evolve. As you become aware of your purpose, proceeding to live with it daily, it transforms continuously within you.

STEP 2 Make a list of your desires in all areas of life. Give yourself free rein, but you must list every desire without guilt or judgment. Remember, what you love is different from other people—otherwise we'd all reach for the same things. If the voice in your head says that your desires are *selfish, impractical, wrong, or bad,* simply answer back, *By whose standard or moral code?* There are rich kings in the Bible, and they are blessed. There are billionaires across the planet, and they, too, are blessed. The key is to seek blessings that are right for you.

When you write down those desires, do so in present tense, but include a target date (I'm striving for "x" by "y" date; I'm driving an "x-model" car by "y" date). According to experts, less than ten percent of individuals actually record their goals, so if you indeed wrote down your desires, you're well ahead of the seven billion other people on the planet. Don't worry if everyone else thinks you're unreasonable—your life is none of their business, and their opinions are none of yours.

STEP 3 After writing down your goals, write **5 actions** that you'll take to turn them into reality. To clarify, I didn't say 5 activities for each goal, but **5 actions** in total. Your list should only contain things that you can execute within seven days. To illustrate, if you have material desires, health desires, and work desires, you could take the following 5 actions:

1. Figure out how much it costs to buy "x."
2. Make a list of your total bank savings or cash.
3. Create a budget.
4. Remove carbs from one meal a day.
5. Come up with a strategy for negotiating a salary increase.

What happens when you write down your desires and take actions to complete them? You start attracting more of what you want—having taken hundreds of steps to get there—and your path emerges suddenly from the fog.

STEP 4 Let's break it down: we wrote down our desires, set target deadlines, identified actions, and took the necessary steps. Now detach from the **meaning** of the result. Admittedly, this is probably the hardest and simplest step. We're responsible for pursuing our goals with all the dedication, discipline, and perseverance we can muster—we do our best and nothing more. Goals inspire us to grow, develop, expand, and transform to meet our targets; our intentions are seeded with a nobility that swells into action.

Therefore, the steps we take should not be judged solely by results, nor by the relationships and environments surrounding us. The forces that drag us down tend to begin in the mind—a problem that plagued me for several years. Whenever I failed to accomplish a goal by a particular date, I'd always judge and assign myself with a negative label. *I am not smart enough, not good enough, not deserving enough, not wise enough, not hardworking enough, etc.* This is not loving behavior but self-abuse, and I was wielding it like a sword.

The purpose of writing down desires is to focus our attention and energy on what we want, rather than harboring regrets about never reaching for our goals. So, write down your desires and ask God to help you achieve them by a certain date. In doing these things, you create a target timeline and thereby focus your actions. If you don't hit the deadline, simply set another one. Learn from what happened and use that insight as a springboard for upcoming actions and goals.

If we hit our targets, excellent; if not, it's time to pull ourselves up and keep on moving. Many times, failure occurs when we attach specific meaning to actions, dividing our lives into areas of achievement and non-achievement. Please, never take this step. Even if you don't meet your goals, you are still excellent. Your goals are important, but they don't define you. The success of contentment is accessible to you at anytime, because you carry memories of past moments when you achieved similar states.

Let's test this theory. Do you have somebody you truly love—a parent, child, or partner? Do you remember a time when you laughed and felt a profound human connection with them, or perhaps a time when you turned a big corner at work, or what about a time when you did something good for someone else, making a difference with a small act? What did you feel then— amazing, successful, worthy? All of these feelings can be triggered at any moment. They are emotions, and accessing them means remembering another time you felt that way. If a goal takes an entire year to complete, we don't have wait 365 days before feeling good again. The days we spend reaching for success are the building blocks of our self-esteem. Embrace action to become a better version of yourself, but do not define yourself by this endgame. You transform your life by giving free rein to desire, because desire alone has the power to unlock the rusted gates of your ambition.

4

The Fourth Pillar of Love is Lighthearedness.

It's much easier to be lighthearted if we stop assigning negative judgments and meanings to things. Anxiety and seriousness come from too much focus on negative outcomes. Just think about it, if you have faith that everything will work out, then why feel anxious? If you are at peace with everything around you, you will feel lighter, not heavy and severe.

Lightheartedness lets you connect with your true self, a place of profound peace and harmony. By being lighthearted, you find humor in situations that otherwise want to pull you down. You have more fun with your life—with events, people, and circumstances. It becomes easier to let go of insults, because you don't take offense or internalize negative feelings. Your defense system learns not to attack itself with intensity or self-judgment.

At five feet tall and about 100 pounds, I often joke with my kids by telling them to call me a little-GIANT. However, I used to struggle with having a sense of humor around them. I'd get too intense and hung-up on the little things, making a big deal about them. I had a notion of what should and shouldn't be and of the distinction between right and wrong. It used to be my way or the *highway*; in my head, I thought I alone knew the right direction.

When we go on holiday, we have to milk every minute and get everything done. We see the sights, participate in everything, and go everywhere. On weekends, we have to get things done, too. Likewise, at work, I decide we must accomplish *this* by *this* date, or I assert my opinions on situations as fact. As you can see, there are too many *shoulds, shouldn'ts, rights,* and *wrongs* in this equation—so heavy and intense! When I take myself too seriously, there's no room for acceptance, appreciation, or desiring with detachment. Everything is attached to something **serious**, and I'm always in the process of scrambling, grasping, and desperately seeking.

In sports, I always notice that the more relaxed person seems to have better flow. Her movements are effortless and elegant; she makes it all look easy. Then there's the other player, who's intense—each shot is harsh, dramatic, and forceful. After a few minutes, the latter player appears tired and stressed, while the former player's prowess seems to crescendo, and she wins with natural ease. While winning is both players' goal, I often sense that the player in flow reaches a state of lightheartedness no matter whether or not she wins.

Just think of movies or plays—when the lead character begins behaving in a severe or obsessed manner, things fall apart. What about the villains, who always seem uptight and stressed? The more uptight they are, the worse they become, and they also don't look right (their features get distorted, things unravel). A person in lightheartedness retains that state no matter what happens around them. She accepts herself, appreciates herself, and desires everything with lightheartedness, because she isn't taking herself too seriously. She takes people, events, or situations for what they seem and does so lightheartedly—no drama, no seriousness, no false backstory to turn everything into a big deal.

She has a desire for people and things because she wants these forces in her life, and she moves towards them with lightheartedness. Cheerful and having fun, she takes action to reach her goals, wants, and desires. If she somehow meets resistance, she continues to flow with lightheartedness towards her next best action. The same is true when she doesn't satisfy her desires on time. Then she'll actually say with a smile, *Okay, that didn't work. What did I learn from this?* She'll live the lesson and choose the next best action.

Having this state of lightheartedness is ideal when it comes to our bodies. To be lighthearted about our bodies, no matter how we look, gives us the power to be, have, and do whatever we want. There are no constraints or hang-ups. The lightheartedness is there, no matter what the weighing scale says. This state is a challenge when you need to control everything and everyone around you. When you feel the need to control a lot of things, you try to micro-manage forces that don't belong to you. If something is "off" even a little bit, you lose your cool, relinquishing control over your emotions and actions. When you live life like this, it's one disappointment after another, because you simply cannot control anyone besides yourself.

What about when you sit there and imagine all the possible worst case scenarios? You have to make sure you cover the bases, but perhaps you don't take action because you're so preoccupied with this illusion of perfection, and all the *what-ifs* along the way. Analysis, paralysis, procrastination, micro-managing, anxiety, and panic attacks: these are the outcomes of wanting everything to be under control, and none of them promote a state of lightheartedness.

The only way to control everything is to become a machine and work only with machines. The moment that you add humanity into the mix, there are a million possibilities of how things will turn out—life becomes strangely human. So what's the point of over-analyzing, overthinking, or being judgemental? Life is uncertain; you can either go with the flow or fight against the current, but we know which of these schools of fish flourish.

You will know that you are acting lightheartedly when there's laughter. Laughter is the best way to channel your energy in a positive direction. Telling jokes about what makes us human is a fantastic boost to our morale. We tend to blow ourselves up, act all important or arrogant, and take personal offense when comments make us insecure. Humor, or telling jokes at our own expense, tends to diffuse all pretense of self-importance and arrogance.

My sister, Christine, has a way of doing this with me whenever I become too intense. One day, I was getting too attached to what people would say when I started writing my book. What if people don't like it or don't like me? Christine simply said, *Even Jesus himself had people who disliked him. What makes you so unique that everyone will like you?* That certainly diffused my moroseness, and I started laughing at myself in the moment. Now, whenever I think about what people will say about me and my book, I remember that conversation.

It's so good to see how ridiculous we are in the grand scheme of things. Whatever we think matters might not, and however we see the future might be vastly incorrect. When I have a sense of humor about my own humanity, I'm saying: *I'm sharing my vulnerabilities, imperfections, and quirks with you! Let's laugh at me together, because I am trusting you with myself.* Poking fun at yourself can be funny and cathartic, because it's often an unexpected way of accepting the unforeseen, forging connections with another human being in the process.

ACTION STEPS!

STEP 1 First, commit to embracing a state of Lightheartedness, especially when you feel heavy or serious. When something complicated happens, your default response should be to smile and laugh, announcing *This is good!* right out of the gates. Focus on what you want (your noble intention) and take action. To incorporate your actions, get out your sticky notes and write: *smile, so the world will smile back at you.* When you remember to smile in all situations, you set yourself up for positive things, because the energy around you begins to glow.

STEP 2 Create two columns in your journal. On the lefthand side, make a list of various times when you took things too seriously, or became too self-critical, beating yourself up or judging yourself harshly. You can write what you said to yourself then in this column. On the righthand side, write down various thoughts, ideas, or actions that could have increased your lightheartedness in those moments. You can even write a joke—come on, give making fun of yourself a try.

STEP 3   Every time you hear yourself debating how things should or shouldn't be, try instead to smile and answer the question: *What do you really want to do?* Your loves and wants are all that should matter to you. Nobody can tell you how to be yourself—unless, of course, your actions cause somebody mental, emotional, or physical harm.

STEP 4   Now take your journal and commit yourself to laughing at these past events. Begin by writing down all the mistakes you made in the past. It might be challenging, but it's time you let go. Laugh at your mistakes and challenges and observe how much you've changed for the better. You are a beautiful living being, full of endless possibilities, so do not strive for perfection. Strive to become truly at peace with yourself.

FREEDOM 5

The Fifth Pillar of Love is Freedom of Self-Expression.

The final pillar is having the freedom to express yourself fully. Once you accept, appreciate, and allow yourself to reach for your desires, you begin living life with lightheartedness and become free to express yourself. Freedom is defined by the Oxford English Dictionary as "the power or right to act, speak, or think as one wants," and it defines "expression" as "the act of making known one's thoughts or feelings."

You have an inner power to speak, think, act, and freely make your thoughts, feelings, and wants known to the world. That internal power is fueled by taking steps to accept and appreciate yourself, desiring without detachment and carrying out actions with lightheartedness. This is excellent, you say, but what about the fears that come up? The good news is.... your fears are your signs. The definition of "sign" by the Oxford English Dictionary is "an object, quality, or event whose presence or occurrence indicates the probable presence or occurrence of something else." Having that fear is thus indicative of the presence or occurrence of something else.

In noticing you have fear, you move forward and create new possibilities! These possibilities are often outside or different from your typical reality, because normal and familiar things don't present fear or obstacles. A pianist doesn't keep playing the same piece—she has to be given more difficult material in order to achieve higher levels of mastery. In the same way, a boxer doesn't keep boxing with the same opponent—he competes in different areas and with different opponents to fine tune his craft. The same is also true for you: if you always know what's coming next and never feel any fear, chances are you're stuck in the same old place doing the same old things. Insanity is defined as doing the same thing over and over again but expecting different results. What if huge fears are preventing you from taking action? If so, it's time to let them go, completely.

My
Story

A young girl was sexually molested between the ages of five and eight years old, by a number of different men: a couple of neighbors, her dad's staff, three cousins, and her uncle. She didn't know what was being done to her, not until she was older, so she never told anybody. How could she complain or protest when she didn't know that the men's actions were wrong? She has memories of being touched in her private parts, of them looming over her and wiping stuff off her skin. She must have trusted those men, for she followed them into a private room, alone.

She also remembers being scared of her grandfather. When she was five years old, she recalls being chased by him with a whip, because she'd played with a water-hose after being told not too. She was so scared of being whipped that she peed in her pants three times; eventually, he caught up to her with his whip. She recalls him hitting and looming over her; at age five, he was so big and threatening that she couldn't find her voice. She didn't have a loving or open relationship with her father at that age. He was usually stern and severe. One day, she asked him for help on some tough homework, but he thought she should figure it out on her own. She felt ashamed that she didn't know the answer and couldn't reason it out. From then on, she decided she had to figure stuff out on her own.

When she was twelve years old, she told a teacher that he was strict with everyone except for one classmate, who was also his niece. The teacher took her to a private room and loomed over her, vowing to ensure that she failed out of school, due to what she'd said. He told her that she wasn't smart enough to be at the school anyways, so she moved to a different school, thinking she was terrible. This girl's experiences with men were often intimidating and scary. This girl was me. It's just easier to talk about it when I distance myself from her.

My experience with men in the workforce was not conducive to free self-expression. Living in the Philippines, I'd assumed a sub-servient role to primarily male bosses, and upon moving to Canada, I worked in a bank dominated by white men. I remember applying for a management trainee position and not getting the job. Eventually, somebody told me in confidence that I'd lost out for being a short Asian woman and therefore not fit for the job. He was right about the short Asian woman part, but it was just his opinion that I wasn't fit for the job. When I shifted careers to the mortgage industry in 2003, it was also dominated by mostly white men, as most industries remain today.

Now let's combine it all. As a young girl, I had experiences of men looming over me, where I felt intimidated and unable to speak up. I believed that I wasn't smart enough growing up, so working in environments where I felt discriminated against or unequal to men felt familiar. I still have such a hard time going toe-to-toe with men or expressing my ideas and opinions fully in their presence—especially BIG men with prominent voices. Distracted thoughts tend to occupy my mind whenever I have face-to-face conversations with men. I feel like they won't listen to me or care what I think. Up until recently, I've had sensations of someone's hand gripping my throat, feeling numb all over as a cold sweat breaks out across my body and the hair on my neck stands up. This usually happens with men, especially when they have voices like booming loudspeakers.

For the longest time, I beat myself up for not speaking up at networking events, especially in the company of men. I worry too much about what "powerful" men might think of me, but I give them a lot of *undeserved* power by believing that they're more successful than me. I attend courses where I'm too scared to speak with the male facilitators. Looking back, I understand why I gravitate towards "gentlemen." My default mode consists of believing that men won't care or listen to me, hence the hand-around-my-throat sensation. Trusting men with my thoughts and opinions is always a challenge, but the bigger and more influential they are, the more they scare me.

How do I use the pillars to express myself better to men? First, I accept that what happened to me in the past *happened* and was not my fault. It's just as easy to make myself into victim as a creator—but I choose the creator. I have risen from the ashes of my past to create a world where I am successful in my own unique way. My life is not over yet; I am still here and willing to create a world of goodness and love, despite everything I've felt in the past.

I appreciate the men in my life right now. My husband and my guy friends are such caring and kind gentlemen. I also appreciate those men who are more difficult for me to open up to and trust, knowing that every time I feel those choking emotions, I'm simply creating a false image in my mind. Instead of empowering that false picture of a monster, I embrace my fear and strive to make a friend. What I resist persists; what I befriend I transcend.

Once I accept or embrace my fear, it becomes my friend, and I can move towards appreciation. As discussed in the previous chapter, there's a noble intention behind every action, as with every fear. My desire is to foster connection and care towards other human beings. When I let that choking sensation overwhelm my body, I make it all about me, rather than focusing on my interaction with the other person. By changing my default position, I can contribute to a small group of people, giving and receiving the gift of connection in turn.

When I focus on being a gift, I become lighthearted. A chat is an opportunity to connect with another human being: period. I say something, and they say something back. I act one way, and they act another. I share my opinion, they share theirs, and all that is enough—no attachments to my opinions being perceived a certain way. I see myself smiling and laughing with everyone, because inside every person, there's a gem waiting to sparkle and expand.

In his book, *The Divine Matrix; Bridging Time, Space, Miracles, and Belief,* Gregg Braden condensed man's universal fears into three headings:

1. **Fear of Separation and Abandonment**: We are afraid of being alone or rejected. We leave relationships or people leave us. This fear also manifests itself in addiction, because we cannot stand being alone, so we turn to social media, TV, drugs, alcohol, etc.

2. **Fear of Low Self-Worth**: This is where we don't feel good enough or smart enough. Impostor syndrome shows up hard here. We feel unworthy of praise, recognition, and compliments. Have you ever been complimented and then felt the need to commend the other person in return? Do you have a hard time embracing their admiration, praise, or benediction? Envy, jealousy, competition, greed, vanity, pride, arrogance, self-doubt, and low self-esteem all come from this universal fear.

3. **Fear of Surrender or Trust**: Not being able to trust people, fear of uncertainty and the unknown, anxiety, worrying, being a control freak, and micro-managing.

What's the use of these fears? For me, knowing that we all have similar fears helps me to feel normal. It's easier to accept and appreciate my fears when I know I'm not alone. We're all facing the same concerns. I can drop the stick—you know, the one I use to beat myself up with every time I'm afraid. We can all drop this stick together, facing our shared fears with lightheartedness and embracing our capacity to act, speak, and fully experience life.

Now that we've recognized such fears, we can acknowledge that underneath them is a desire for love. When we love ourselves, we're okay with being alone; we feel worthy and trust ourselves completely. When our fears are transcended, they lead us back to self-love.

Summary

Fear is the biggest obstacle we face in expressing ourselves fully. Now that we know our pillars, we can use them to complete the circle.

The First Pillar is Acceptance: So you have this fear—it's not good or bad, but you must not reject its presence. Commit to accepting the fear instead, and notice how it often precipitates an action. You are not required to get rid of the fear before taking action, for that way you may never act. Instead, discover which of the top universal fears you are experiencing. Maybe it's a combination of all three? What is the noble intention, or what desire is lurking behind this fear? Is it achievement, excellence, connection, or perhaps sharing? Next, focus on love and repeat *I love myself, I love myself, I love myself* for one minute. Zoom in and focus on your intention.

How do you know if you're making up stories about adverse outcomes or future results? Probably because you're too paralyzed by fear to get started. There are an infinite number of possible outcomes or scenarios—is trying to predict them a good use of your time? What if you stopped this inner dialogue and just gave things a shot? Be open and curious about the possibilities. Remember, life will continue to evolve and flow, with all its glorious possibilities, provided you let it.

<u>The Second Pillar is Appreciation:</u> What can you appreciate about fear? What are the values behind your experience of it, and do they accord with noble intentions? I appreciate knowing that I don't want to be rejected, because it teaches me that I value connection. I can increase my level of connection by acting or expressing myself despite my fears, creating new possibilities for contact. This communication makes me appreciate my connection with another human being and fuels future intimacy as well. I appreciate understanding that my distaste for feeling unintelligent comes from favoring mastery and excellence. I can increase my intellectual proficiencies by taking on new habits and skills, learning new things as I go, instead of waiting around for perfection.

<u>The Third Pillar is Desire with Detachment:</u> You have a goal, a dream, or an ambition, but you let fear become an obstacle to reaching it. Fear of rejection means you're committing to ask for something. Fear of not being smart enough means you're embarking on something new and challenging. Focus on the desire instead. You want what you want; you desire what you desire; you love what you love. It's okay if people find you unreasonable. It's okay if they don't get it at first. If you don't ask, the answer is always "no." By asking and taking action, you create space for what you want. Your chances of making it happen increase tenfold. Try to notice how your desires have a way of benefitting others. The larger the dream, the more significant the team. Your team could be your family, your friends, your co-workers, your relatives...basically anyone around you. We are all interconnected. As you elevate yourself and create more possibilities for life, you promote other people's lives too.

<u>The Fourth Pillar is Lightheartedness:</u> Did you notice that whenever you focus on your fears, they become bigger and more menacing? The longer you sit with them, the more they morph into giants. If you then start making up false narratives with negative outcomes, reaching lightheartedness becomes impossible. Do you move with a spring in your step, with all that negative self-talk weighing you down? What if you focus on lightheartedness instead? How you can make this moment more lighthearted? Personally, I start by unloading my fears. I imagine the big scary monster as a white wolf friend beside me, and I repeatedly chant: *lighthearted, lighthearted, lighthearted.* Energy flows wherever attention goes. I think of loving myself—I think about what I want and take the next best action. I choose easy, lighthearted actions, ready to spring onwards to the next step, until eventually I've made a giant leap.

<u>The Fifth Pillar is Freedom to Express Myself Fully:</u> Those lighthearted steps and actions give way to full expression. Making the next move and speaking up are easier when I have lightheartedness in my heart, rather than carrying the burden of fear and worry. When I accept and appreciate all of myself, including my fears, when I commit to my desires with detachment, when I'm lighthearted through my core, I love myself fully. I feel free to express myself, open to experiencing things honestly—minute by minute, hour by hour—both in private and around others. I **D.A.R.E:** **D** for Desire, **A** for Act, **R** for Receive, and **E** for Express. Yes, because I love myself, I D.A.R.E.

When you love yourself, you fill reservoirs of kindness, care, and support. You accept you are human and prone to making mistakes. You'll never be quick to judge yourself harshly, but rather to forgive and feel happier with yourself. It's a really beautiful thing, this magic trick of loving ourselves.

Loving
Others

PART TWO

LOOKING BEYOND YOURSELF

Now that you're practicing self-love, notice how your love for others naturally flows outwards from you. Just a reminder, we've been discussing the Bible's expression of love under **1 Corinthians 13:4-8. "Love is patient; love is kind. It does not envy; it does not boast; it is not proud. It does not dishonor others; it is not self-seeking, it is not easily angered, it keeps no record of wrongs. Love does not delight in evil but rejoices with the truth. It always protects, always trusts, always hopes, always perseveres. Love never fails."**

Let us experience love in the behaviors you're already practicing for yourself. According to Brian Tracy, "80% of life satisfaction comes from meaningful relationships." If you want more happiness in life, you must give more of yourself to the people surrounding you. How do you give more of you? By giving them your love. How do you give them more love? When you practice the 5 Pillars: Acceptance, Appreciation, honoring their Desires with Detachment, Lightheartedness, and allowing them Freedom of Self-Expression. Since you're practicing these pillars on yourself, we can now create a possibility for expanding this towards others.

ACCEPTANCE TOWARDS OTHERS **6**

Life's Wonderful Gifts to Other People.

Do you recall the meaning of acceptance? In Chapter 1, we discovered that the purpose of acceptance is to receive willingly, while giving approval to and accepting relationships and circumstances as reality. True acceptance lies not only in accepting yourself, but in embracing every part of another person from head to toe—their physical self, their ways of being, their actions and modes of communication—seeing everything that makes them who they are. In other words, we do not reject or judge others negatively for thinking, talking, feeling, or acting differently from us.

Most importantly, we make a stand and claim them as our own. They belong to us. You may argue that you do not really own these people, and it's true that you don't own them physically, but bear this in mind: you own something a lot more when you experience 100% of it. Why do certain people like each other, while other people might not? Why do children have different connections with their mothers and fathers compared to their siblings? For one thing, the experience of the parents is unique for each of the siblings. No two individuals are alike, each person is unique, therefore how they experience each other is different when they actually interact with others.

So, the first phase of loving someone unconditionally is to acknowledge that this person is yours. You own your experience of him or her 100%. Your mother, father, spouse, each of your children, your friends, your relatives, and acquaintances: they are yours in practice, because you are the source of all your experiences. To take it a step further, out of all the mothers and fathers out there, you ended up with who you did. Out of all the billions of children in the world, you have *your* children. Out of all the billions of people alive, you ended up with *your* relatives, friends, staff, boss, etc.

What if you took on the role of a powerful being and chose your loved ones to play on your team? What if you intentionally picked the people in your life with whom you could learn and love? What would they teach you? In life, my best teachers are often those individuals who I struggle with most of all. The funny truth is that until I learn the lesson, they keep coming back to teach me. Is this notion even possible? Are the people in my life here as my teachers? When somebody asks that question, I always say that anything is possible. Even a 0.0000000001% probability means there is a possibility.

Besides, consider the alternative: the people in your life just randomly showed up out of the blue, with no rhyme or reason; everybody just showed up on this planet to exist and occupy a small spot of earth. That means that all our moments of happiness, love, joy, struggle, success, triumph, and wisdom were random coincidences. I don't see any responsibility, power, love, or joy in that. When you look at this, life assumes a random component and is therefore not beautiful. I for one adopt only ideas and concepts that inspire creativity, authority, responsibility, and above all, happiness. Therefore, the previous theory is my point of reference. I believe that I magically choose the people in my life. Why don't you wear that hat for a while, try it on? In other words, look at everybody around you as a teacher and see how things change.

When you find negative people in your life, say to yourself, *there is no way I would have chosen these people; they are mean, selfish, arrogant, cold, disrespectful, uncaring, unsupportive, self-righteous,* or whatever. If these people are verbally and physically abusive, I suggest you get help *now.* For the rest of the population, I understand that your experience of certain people might not be 100% pleasant, but I wonder if you are 100% pleasant in all your dealings with them. After all, there's more than one person in a relationship, and you don't know how the other person is experiencing you. You may be showing up as the same person you label them to be. Remember that childhood taunt, *it takes one to know one*? How do you recognize selfishness if you haven't been selfish? How do you recognize disrespect if you haven't been disrespectful? Carl Jung said that "the information that is most unconscious in us, we, by need, must project it out onto someone around us. We must by need, project it out onto people or events around us. So the fact is, we really can't see anything other than who we are." What I'm saying here, as with the age old childhood taunt, is that this person is your mirror—what you see is you.

Let's examine a scenario in which one sister refuses to share with her brother. One might say that she's selfish, while another might see this as an opportunity to teach her about sharing. Someone else might think that she's hungry, another person might see her brother as too lazy to get his own or simply opportunistic, and someone else might think that she wants attention. We can do this forever—all sorts of judgments, labels, and stories can emerge from one incident.

On another occasion, a teenager speaks out to her mom, raising her voice significantly, because she's a little emotional. One might say she's being disrespectful for speaking her mind, another might see that she's asking for something she needs, while others might believe that she's scared, troubled, angry, confident, courageous, or even whiny.

Finally, labeling somebody as selfish, disrespectful, or manipulative is not really fair. When you do that, you act like this person behaves that way 24/7. Can somebody be 100% selfish all the time? Funny, we often have this excellent way of making a statement and finding ways to prove that statement. "He is selfish... See, he did this and that," and the next thing you know, you keep talking about all the things he did that were selfish. In the meantime, you ignore lots of other moments when he behaved differently.

Despite this external person in your life, you are the source of your own experience. No matter what happened with them or who's to blame, you likely processed that occurrence subjectively in your head. In Neuro-Linguistic Programming, this is called Internal Representation. When an event occurs, you delete, distort, and generalize the information based on your past experiences, values, beliefs, programming, and knowledge sets. All of this happens subconsciously in split seconds.

To demonstrate, pause for a minute and look around you. For about thirty seconds, pick out everything that is black, and make a note of how many black objects you see. Okay, now close your eyes again. Can you remember how many objects were red and blue? Open your eyes and look around—do there now appear to be more red and blue objects than black objects? Most likely, your brain initially filtered out anything red and blue, temporarily deleting, distorting, and generalizing, back when black was your focus. It may have seemed that the red and blue objects were sparsely there, but in reality, they were just waiting to be seen.

A similar process occurs in your mind when you interact with people. As you process events in your head, you are technically creating a little movie or story in your mind. After you've filtered through all of that, creating your own story, you can then label the occurrence as "x." That, in turn, becomes your reality. I say "yours" because we all filter things differently in our minds, based on our own mental programming. Your feelings will organize themselves into a story, or your version of reality, and before you know it, you add a title to that movie—a generalized label to name the occurrence and person. You create all that on your own, out of the stories in your mind that insist on being reality, and from that creation, you act in a certain way, which drives your results and sometimes the entire pattern of your life.

Let's go back to the example of a teenager talking to her mother, where the sound of her voice was louder than usual. When the mother sees, hears, and experiences her daughter talking in this manner, she deletes, distorts, and generalizes what she understands based on her own experiences, beliefs, values, and morals. Perhaps she then labels her daughter's communication as disrespectful. What do you think she'll feel then? She will act out of anger, resentment, and hurt, likely electing to yell back at her daughter, as her mind is overwhelmed with emotion.

On the other hand, if she labels her daughter's communication as assertive and independent, she might feel proud, compassionate, or curious. Her actions will be much different then, and she'll create a higher quality relationship than previously possible. When you give your attention to something, you invest your energy. The feelings and thoughts residing in that energy determine the quality of your relationships, and since you create your experiences with others, you alone have the power to forge meaningful connections.

On an individual scale, it starts with claiming the other person as your **no. 1 choice**, owning your experience of them in every single moment and ultimately choosing the design of your relationship. The next piece lies in taking 100% responsibility for the relationship. In Al Ritter's book, *The 100/0 Principle: The Secret of Great Relationships,* he suggests that you "take full responsibility (the 100) for the relationship, expecting nothing (the 0) in return."

Responsibility means having the awareness, power, and control to respond to any situation however you want. You can create a response to your situation and the people around you. To exercise this enormous power, you remove blame from the equation—there's no, *he made me mad, he made me sad, he made me angry, he annoyed me, he hurt me, etc.* That is not taking responsibility but giving away your personal power. Your mind will say, *You don't understand, he did this to me.* Yes, he *did*, but it's in the past. You can't carry that around with you, but you can respond in a way that gives you the personal power to evolve and mature.

Let's look at being a partner, wife, or husband. First, we have to accept our role as partner. *I am a wife, I choose to be a wife, and I own my "wifeness," rather than joining the millions of lonely people without partners.* From that place of ownership and responsibility, I create my own value. I value my loving connection, my understanding, and my generosity, and I can appreciate my loving relationship when I choose to be kind, rather than insisting on being right. I appreciate my value of understanding when my husband talks about his work. I appreciate my value of generosity when I cook us my favorite food. As I take action to increase or appreciate my values of connection, understanding, and generosity, it thus follows that I appreciate my "wifeness" and role as his partner.

What about my achievements? So far, I've achieved a specific position and salary at work. If I focus on other people having more than me, I will not appreciate my achievements. Instead, I embrace what I've accomplished; I choose it, I own it. I value excellence, mastery, and success, so I take action to appreciate these values.

My value of excellence increases when I take courses, read, or improve my craft. I appreciate my value of mastery by training to enhance my skills. I enjoy my success through setting goals and creating plans to achieve them. As I take action to increase excellence, mastery, and success, I understand my career path all the more. Accepting these areas of my life makes this process easy. In a sense, all we have to do is learn to accept, just as the Serenity Prayer Suggests:

"God grant me the serenity
to accept the things I cannot change;
courage to change the things I can;
and wisdom to know the difference."

You cannot change someone else's actions. You can accept that things happened as they did; choose your response and create possibilities from that reality. You have the power to let moments either energize or drain you. By taking responsibility, you actually stimulate your personal energy. By taking responsibility for relationships, we embrace and accept people 100%, ceasing to give them negative judgments and false expectations in return.

Another strategy is to become an "inverse paranoid" like W. Clement Stone. Instead of believing that someone or something was out to harm him, he believed that everyone was plotting to do him good. He tended to look at everyone and everything as complicit in some conspiracy to help him become more successful. What if you saw everyone and everything happening around you as a gift or blessing? What kind of life would that be, if everyone around you embodied grace waiting to be discovered? This is probably why the now is called the present. What's happening now is designed to help you realize your own goodness. All you have to do is accept.

ACTION STEPS!

STEP 1 Look at every single relationship that you have and make a list (your parents, grandparents, siblings, kids, in-laws, relatives, friends, co-workers, and clients).

STEP 2 Beside their name, write statements such as, *Mom, I choose to accept all of you.* Write this down beside every person's name. How does it feel to accept these relationships as yours, knowing that out of over seven billion human beings in the world, you created a relationship with these individuals?

STEP 3 When you're feeling resistance, negativity, or conflict, repeat this to yourself, *I am responsible for all of my experiences with people.* This means you choose how to respond to whatever is occurring right now. The best way to generate a reaction that works is always seeking nobility in your actions and relationships. As discussed in the previous chapter, noble intentions lie behind our actions, comments, desires, and ambitions. Be an **"inverse paranoid"** and see how this person or experience is a gift to you.

STEP 4 Stop yourself whenever you imagine a negative outcome, result, or judgment. Avoid creating false endings, which only diminish the flow of possibilities. Every day, tell yourself repeatedly, *I believe that something beautiful is going to happen to me today.* No matter what happens, no matter how everyone else behaves, keep saying this to yourself. You'll be amazed at how you're more comfortable accepting everyone and everything around you— how energized and enthusiastic you are in every way.

APPRECIATION OF OTHERS 7

Delight in the many blessings that surround you.

Once we commit to practicing 100% acceptance towards other people, we are ready to appreciate them. In Chapter 2, we discovered that things appreciate *in value* upon feeding them positive attention. We also saw how complaining about something often causes negative energy and intensity to build around that thing, thus driving negative appreciation.

Let's take the example of an unsupportive spouse. Upon noticing this trait, our nervous system rears its ugly head, and we find more stories, data, and proof of its validity, thereby giving value to the possibility. The more we suggest that someone is unsupportive, the more this feeling appreciates within ourselves, and perhaps we even take action based on that thought. The thought becomes a self-fulfilling prophecy. Let's say your husband behaves unsupportively by neglecting to help you with a project. What do you do then? If you respond by acting in equally unsupportive ways yourself, giving him the cold shoulder or speaking to him unpleasantly, he might not offer the exact support you need. He will be so turned off by your behavior that he'll send the same energy back, feeling that *you* are the unsupportive one. What you have just done is increase or appreciate the value of your unsupportive spouse.

You might see the same thing happening with your kids. Once you decide that your child is irresponsible, lazy, or disrespectful, you find more events or data points to reinforce your story. You act in ways that fulfill your expectation, thereby appreciating what you appreciate. If your child is irresponsible, you might nag or criticize him for not cleaning his room, but he's only a child. On the other hand, he might feel that you, as the adult, are being disrespectful of his space. If you lose your temper with him, he might feel hurt and insulted, proceeding to retaliate with his own tantrum. In this situation, you empower your negative feelings and those of your child.

What about at work? What do you appreciate about your colleagues? Have you ever labeled them as procrastinators, lazy, disorganized, irresponsible, slow, hasty, micromanagers, mean, or disrespectful? How often do you fuel the fire? Do the flames lick the edges of your life the more you appreciate these negative traits? The people around you are mirrors reflecting what you choose to see. The more negativity you feel, the more negativity you attract, and the more negativity you ultimately exude.

As with your colleagues, you're only human, so chances are you've procrastinated or acted lazy in the past yourself. You may be organized in one area but not in another. You may have acted irresponsibly at some point in time. If you are an energizer bunny, there may still be areas in life where you're slow. When you look at yourself, do you *always* act in these ways? Not really, but you have your moments. The same is true with the people around you; they have their moments, too, and at different moments than you, so which moment and trait will you ultimately choose to appreciate? How then do we stop ourselves from this cycle of negative appreciation? We go back to the very beginning. We recall that satisfaction means to value something or recognize its full worth, and then we increase those forces in our lives.

ACTION STEPS!

STEP 1   We made a relationship list in Chapter 6. Using this list, discover the values you want out of each relationship. For example, upon accepting your mother 100%, what values do you appreciate in your relationship with her? For me, I value caring, deep connection, nurturing, support, and understanding when it comes to my mother. For my spouse and kids, I value the same things, but I add fun and laughter into the mix as well. I love creating moments of joy on a daily basis, whether they're laughing at me, or with me. I love it when they tease, mock, and make fun of me, because it shows that they're comfortable enough to see my humanity.

STEP 2   List one action you'll take this week to appreciate your values. For example, the importance of understanding— what will it take to give this particular person more understanding? Notice that I said *give*: the act of increasing what's already there. Remember the 100/0 relationship principle? You give 100% without the intention of receiving anything back. When you give with zero expectations of receiving, something wonderful happens: you get things back a hundredfold. If you keep offering other people understanding, they will behave in a more understanding way towards you. If you focus on caring and appreciation, you'll likely feel cared for and appreciated by others. You do reap what you sow; the universe rewards you for appreciation in many ways.

STEP 3 Review this list as a reminder of the important values and actions to which you're committed. As you execute and cross off various actions, notice how your feelings of appreciation expand inside you. Be grateful, because you're taking on more of the values you've listed. You are becoming more caring, connected, nurturing, loving, understanding, supportive, and fun. In your act of giving, you are actually receiving.

DESIRING FOR OTHERS
WITH DETACHMENT

8

*Crave to transform your desires
without fear or favor.*

In Chapter 3, you gave yourself the freedom to desire what you
desire. If somebody read your list, would they understand why
you desire such things for yourself? You have your own purpose,
ideals, beliefs, experiences, and values; perhaps reading your list
is akin to translating from a different language. No matter how
many hours of explanation or justification you might be able to
provide, they may never feel the same desire inside themselves,
and that is okay. You are not required to defend your desires to

anyone—just accept and appreciate yourself, with all your inner wishes, hopes, and dreams.

What about the people around you? Think about your parents, kids, siblings, and close friends—what do they want in their lives? Do you honor their desires or judge them as unreasonable? Congratulations, they are just like you. You are irrational to them when it comes to your desires, so why should their desires be reasonable to you?

I love taking courses, training, and reading books. One year, I spent over $50,000 on these exercises. I told myself it was okay, because I become a better person when I learn, using my learning to grow my business. Furthermore, by becoming a better person, I can make a positive lasting difference in the lives of my family and friends. I'm striving to be more excellent, masterful, and prosperous—these courses help me get there. Meanwhile, my husband loves gadgets and new technology. He'll buy the latest devices and the most recent apps. My son loves video games, and my daughter loves to hang out with her boyfriend, who I long believed was not good enough for her. After going through some serious introspection, I realized that I was judging their desires as inferior to mine!

I felt resentful when my husband spent his money on technology, because it's composed of material "things," unlike my books or courses. Every time Amazon shows up on our doorstep, I become judgmental and think, *There he goes again, getting attached to trivial things and wasting his money.* He not only wanted the latest iPhone for Christmas, but also the iWatch, so I told him he didn't need both—just get one. I also judged my son's video games as a waste of time, thinking he should be reading and pursuing higher knowledge, rather than investing in worthless games and toys. For Christmas, he wanted two toys, so I told him to decide which one he really needed. My daughter doesn't buy a lot of stuff, but she loves to hang out with her boyfriend and friends from school. They tend to sit around the house watching hours of TV, and I always judged this as a waste of time. I limited the amount of time she spent with her boyfriend, announcing that I didn't want to be home if he came over.

Basically, I judged their desires as trivial and foolish, even though my books and courses were also just *things*, especially from their perspective. They don't understand my desires, nor my relentless pursuit of knowledge. I realized that my desires were unreasonable to them; I was being too self-righteous. I simply had no acceptance or appreciation for what they desired. How could I learn to support them without accepting and appreciating their values? This thought grew into a personal epiphany, and I took action to change things, committing my mind to accepting their unique desires. They like what they like; they desire what they desire; they love what they love. We are all human beings with unique needs and wants.

I must recognize that appreciating values consists of something different for my family members. I talked to my husband and agreed to appreciate the value of what's important to him. I said that he could have both devices, and I wouldn't say a word, acknowledging that I'd already spent thousands of dollars on personal training, so who was I to judge my things as better than his? I acknowledged that I'd been acting with self-righteous indignation and stepped back from the toxicity of that feeling.

With my son, I honored what he wanted, spending time trying to understand his video games and buying him the toys he wanted. Meanwhile, I told my daughter that I'd misjudged her boyfriend. He had made one negative comment and I'd used it to invalidate all of his prior actions, when really he was just your typical teenager. I'd seen a text on her phone, in which he'd called adults "big stupid" and pressured our daughter into being dishonest. In reality, I probably caused both of them to hide the truth, because of my self-righteous air, so I said he was free to come over whenever he wanted. I appreciated that they liked spending time in our home, and now she feels free to be honest with me about her plans, knowing that I won't judge her desires as inferior to mine.

The actions I took with my family led to deeper connections at home. Meanwhile, I learned to use the same approach with my friends and clients. Now I have a deeper appreciation for everybody's desires. I listen to what's important to them and help them achieve their goals. I have a sense of wonder and fascination in listening to them talk about their dreams, which changes the way I see the world. I encourage you to adopt the same mindset. Zig Ziglar said it best: "You can have everything you want, if you will just help other people get what they want."

When I supported my family in their desires, guess what happened? They offered respect and support for my desires as well, rather than thinking I was weird for pursuing my own goals. If you want more acceptance from others, make the first move. If you want more appreciation, appreciate more things. If you want more respect, show more respect. If you want more affection, shower your loved ones with that same delight. If you want understanding, start learning to understand.

ACTION STEPS!

STEP 1 Return to the list from Chapter 7. Look at the people you've chosen to accept and appreciate—can you remember a time when they expressed a desire or dream, and you helped them achieve that goal? How did that make you feel? What about the desires or dreams that you thought were unreasonable, weird, or impossible? Do you see them differently now?

STEP 2 Knowing that everyone's desires are unique in many ways, can you help other people create a world from their hearts' desires? Think of specific individuals in your life and brainstorm ways to support their deepest wants and needs. Sometimes, the biggest step in helping someone is to realize what kind of help they seek.

STEP 3 Finally, detach from the result. Practice the 100/0 Principle and keep giving with zero expectations. If you do this, the act of giving will bring you joy. Kahlil Gibran said, "I slept and dreamt that life was joy. I awoke and saw that life was service. I acted and behold, service was joy." When you make other people's desires, wants, needs, or dreams as necessary as your own, you discover that other people, God, and the Universe do the same thing for you.

Be happy,
blessings abound!

As you practice acceptance, appreciation, and desiring on behalf of yourself and others, reaching a state of lightheartedness becomes easy. At this point, you have less baggage to carry around, having relinquished your negative judgments and unfair expectations of other people. You accept and appreciate them as individuals instead, considering and respecting their unique values, while doing the same thing for yourself.

In a consistent state of lightheartedness, it's natural to laugh—at yourself and along with others. Taking other people too seriously is the easiest route to taking yourself too seriously. It's easy to be lighthearted when you detach from depressing judgments and stories. Most of the time, this state of lightheartedness is disrupted by your ego. The Oxford English Dictionary defines *ego* as "a person's self-esteem or self-importance." Your ego is how you see yourself and how you want to be seen, but such self-importance is layered with judgments, biases, and prejudices. We all have our own definitions of right versus wrong, good versus bad, beauty versus ugliness.

Most of the time, when you feel negative emotions like anger, disappointment, frustration, loneliness, sadness, or fear, the present moment is grinding against your personal views of right and wrong, or against your sense of self-importance and the external persona you present to the world. If the situation involves another person, your perception is probably rooted in believing that they've failed to show up for you, or even intentionally done you wrong. However, when you remember that there are multiple ways to see, feel, and interpret situations in your life, it's easier to consider another person's unique perspective.

According to the Encyclopedia Britannica, "the human mind processes eleven million bits of information every second." It deletes, distorts, and generalizes such information, creating different networks of thought, which inform our views on the world. Understanding that everyone processes information differently, it follows that everyone should have their own unique point of view. For all we know, this diversity of thought is precisely what makes the great world go round and round again.

Let's take *sand,* for instance. How to hold a handful of sand? The tighter you hold the sand, the more it spills over, leaving less to appreciate and enjoy. What about water? Do you attempt to clutch water with your fist, or do you open your palms and let it pool inside? Achieving a state of lightheartedness comes from openness. We hold more when we open our palms. Likewise, when our hearts are open to numerous possibilities, we nurture our relationships with meaning and beauty, ready to embrace a brand new galaxy of perspective. However, in clinging to one way of thinking about things, we start gripping the world too tight. We lose relationships and reduce the possibility of creating happiness or wonder in our lives. When we take our own point of view too seriously—when self-importance gets the best of us—there's no room for lightheartedness anymore.

ACTION STEPS!

STEP 1   Make a list of your hot buttons—the things, people, events, or patterns that trigger negative feelings or reactions in you. Remember, you're not making this list to judge or abuse yourself. Be free to connect with your inner self when writing this list. It exists for you and no one else.

STEP 2   Look at your list and find the humor or ridiculousness behind the meanings you've attached to these triggers. It may seem difficult at first, but with every step, moving forward becomes easier. Laugh and embrace the folly of your list. Remember, do not let negative emotions cloud your thoughts about old moments—we are about to recreate your picture of these events.

STEP 3   Create a funny story about these moments, finding a way to poke fun at yourself. Laugh, beckoning forward a state of lightheartedness, rather than frustration and negativity.

STEP 4 Add humor and laughter to the list from Chapter 8, as you'd like to experience more joy with loved ones. When you seek and project humor in your relationships, you increase the value of those connections, and people gravitate towards you like long lost magnets.

STEP 5 Commit to evoking laughter and joy in every interaction, and notice how good this makes you feel. Strive to make others feel lighthearted. Learn not to take offense at other people's opinions; instead, accept them with an effusive smile. In doing so, profound joy becomes your watchword. The meaning of a successful relationship takes on a new definition, incorporating more acceptance, appreciation, and ultimately love for others.

10

Learn to make space for another's self-expression.

When you accept, appreciate, and support the desires of others with lightheartedness, everyone around you has the freedom to express themselves fully—this is an experience of unconditional love. When you ask someone about a charming acquaintance, you typically hear stories about how they made other people feel. When you are open towards other people, they feel comfortable reciprocating the same openness, knowing how much they matter to you. That attitude and charisma can be developed over time— all you need do is take the necessary steps. You can only be truly successful when you let others feel "wanted' around you. In doing this, you contribute not just to yourself, but to their lives.

When I think about the people who helped me become who I am today, I don't remember their accomplishments or expertise, not even their words of reassurance about my goals. What I think about most is their sincere belief in me. They let me know—through their actions, words, and unspoken thoughts—that I matter. It's the same with the people in your life; they need validation because they matter to you in every way. You have accepted them and learned to gravitate towards their desires. Now it's time to use expression as a tool for compassionate reciprocation.

ACTION STEPS!

STEP 1   Let those around you feel comfortable enough to express themselves freely. Learn to listen and really see the value in their inner worlds. It's crucial that they share their thoughts with you. Give them your attention and do not be quick to judge them. According to Jessica Stillman, before you go into any conversation, say to yourself, "I am not going to take the spotlight."

STEP 2   Let this person feel flattered; appreciate them in speech and behavior. Let them capture your entire interest. Do not make them feel ignorant or foolish, as if your knowledge is more important than their thoughts. Even when it feels like you know more, learn to listen to their point of view.

STEP 3   To let someone know you are interested in them, engage by asking questions about them. Sometimes we grapple for the right questions, but when you take time to listen, what they say gives you the road. Ask them questions when they challenge your assumptions, and feel your heart swell as your perspective embraces more of the world.

STEP 4 What body language is used around you? Invest in conversations by letting the other person feel like the epicenter of your world. Eliminate distractions and point your body towards them. Let every part of you tell them, *I am interested rather than I am distracted and nervous or I am better than you.* Ensure that you maintain eye contact. Last but not least, smile. Let this person see that you're entirely interested in them.

Summary

Let's try out these strategies on some common life occurrences.

Your daughter comes home late. You all agreed that she'd be home by 10pm, but she doesn't arrive until 11pm.

The First Pillar is Acceptance: Okay, she came home at 11pm. You cannot change that. You can choose to accept your daughter as your daughter. You can choose to accept this situation and be responsible for your emotions. You can choose how to respond. If you criticize her actions and the situation overall, you cannot move to the next pillar of appreciation. Remember that you have to embrace and accept 100% of this moment before you can appreciate your daughter.

The Second Pillar is Appreciation: Focus on creating appreciation by enhancing the positive value of this event. If you focus on negative narratives and feelings, you'll only appreciate the value of those sentiments. Is that what you want to appreciate? What exactly are you valuing by wanting her home at 10am? Is it her safety? Is it your sense of discipline or respect? You have to be clear about why you're attaching such importance to her lateness. Often, we're concerned about our children's safety, but here she is, safe and sound, so what's the problem? Learn to appreciate her safety and conquer the second pillar.

The Third Pillar is Desire: On your earlier list, you wrote down what values were important with regard to your daughter. Whether it's respect, understanding, appreciation, deep connection, or unconditional love, focus on that value and give her what you wish to receive back. Typically, we react to disrespect by demanding the opposite, acting very self-righteous and preaching dogma to the clouds. How's that working for you? Will it attract what you want or simply drive a deeper wedge? If you desire more respect from your daughter, try sitting down first and giving her the respect that she deserves. By allowing for open and honest communication, you inherently foster more respect in your relationship. Using your list of values, identify what actions you can take to give your daughter what you seek.

The Fourth Pillar is Lightheartedness: She came back one hour late, and now she's in for the night. If you let go of your feelings of self-importance and seriousness, can you see the humor in this situation? *Come on, Mom—she's home!* Plus, there are millions of possible scenarios to explain why she's late. She probably didn't go out of her way to piss you off, but if she did, maybe you contributed to creating that type of relationship dynamic. Remember, everything is your responsibility 100/0. Start laughing at the ridiculousness of your self-narratives and approach her with your hang-ups.

The Fifth Pillar is Full Freedom of Expression: Now that you've achieved lightheartedness, you can lightly express the stories you've fabricated in your mind. Remember to share what's truly important to you about your relationship. If you talk to your daughter in a lighthearted manner, she'll likely be more open to telling you what's actually happening, rather than lying. By truly giving yourself the freedom to express your thoughts and values, you give her the freedom to do the same.

Now, let's examine this from the perspective of your spouse. It's typical for wives to multi-task and take on more at home, thereby creating an environment where our spouses don't help around the house, and we resent them in turn. How do we end up in these situations? For one thing, we start out in the honeymoon stage and love doing everything for our partners. When they want to help (because they, too, are in the honeymoon stage), we often say, "It's okay, I can do this."

Over time, they stop offering to help, or they plow ahead without asking and it doesn't get done your way. Perhaps you make some sarcastic remark or redo their work—at this point, you cannot blame them for leaving the chores to you. As you have more kids and responsibilities—and life inevitably gets bigger—you reach a state of overwhelm. Meanwhile, your husband continues to strike you as unhelpful and unsupportive, but you have created the nature of your relationship, and you are responsible for changing how people treat you.

ACTION STEPS!

Let's say your husband is not cleaning up the kitchen after dinner. (In short your husband is not doing or being enough.)

The First Step is to Accept your husband 100%. Accept 100/0 responsibility for this relationship.

The Second and Third Steps: Appreciate, desire, and remember the values from your list. What values correlate to him helping you after dinner? Are you looking for more support, intimacy, or nurturing attention? If you want more support, figure out how you can support him first, and then notice how your support comes back to you. When this happens, say to your spouse, "Thank you, I like feeling supported when you do *x*." Keep giving support and appreciation when you experience the same support from him. By doing this, you channel more energy into his willingness to be supportive, because you're giving him that same attention.

Remember, we delete millions of data-bytes and pieces of information from our memories, keeping only what's necessary. It's probably not hard to find more examples of him being unsupportive than supportive, but the more you appreciate what you appreciate, the more you create more of those elements in your life. Try going out of your way to do something special for him, keeping in mind that his desires might vary at different times of day.

The Fourth Step is Lightheartedness: Stop internalizing your feelings of martyrdom and victimization. Look for humor in whatever you're clinging to so tightly, and try to see the ridiculousness of the situation. Find the laughing points, dropping your baggage and attachments in favor of lightness. Focus on recalling moments or narratives in which your husband was caring.

The Fifth Step is Freedom of Self-Expression: Open up by sharing your story and whatever you're working to change. Perhaps try doing this after you've successfully taken steps one to three for a couple of weeks. By then, you'll be used to adopting opposing actions to your automatic modes of being, and your spouse will see that you've relinquished some old patterns and want to improve your relationship—one where everyone takes responsibility for their actions. When you share this with him, remember the "100/0" principle and expect zero in return. There are many ways for him to respond, so be open to them all.

In Chapter Five, we talked about the three universal fears. All human beings experience these fears. Our spouse, kids, family, friends, relatives, and colleagues may all struggle to speak freely, so when people *act out* around you, choose to see that moment as them feeling free to express themselves. Maybe their actions or words are not exactly what you want, but you're creating space for them to be themselves, and that's a gift with positive value.

I believe that there's pain or fear behind every moment of anger, defensiveness, violence, or negativity, but behind every pain or fear, there's also the desire for love. The silent expectation of love takes subtle forms, like understanding, caring, nurturing, support, and compassion. If you give everyone the freedom to act, speak, and experience life on their own terms, you're giving them a tremendous gift. Just imagine, if you unbind them from the shackles of negative judgments, fears, pains, and doubts, what might they accomplish?

Your gifts of acceptance, appreciation, compassionate desire, lightheartedness, and freedom of expression give them the power to be. You are a gift to all human beings, and all human beings are a gift to you. Most importantly, you are a gift to you. You have only one job in this world: expand these gifts from yourself to others, and do so generously.

Life

PART THREE

AN INTERLUDE FROM
THE AUTHOR

Every step we take in life must begin with a robust framework, like a building that stands against the weather of challenge, blame, rejection, and mockery. Life on earth is fragile and vulnerable to the dictates of society. When you let life unravel without a solid foundation, it withers away, blown by the stormy all-encompassing winds of this world, but when firmly rooted, we stand strong with friends and foes alike. It's important to build your life's foundation with the elements that matter most.

You have taken the first and second steps; you are practicing how to love yourself and others. Now it's time to enjoy your life, with all its myriad flaws and strengths. You must achieve this through the five pillars. Nurture appreciation for your position in life and learn to bestow this appreciation on others. Know that work completed with purpose and integrity is more rewarding, and ask yourself the question, *Do your beliefs bring you joy?* In this next and final section, we will inaugurate the five foundational pillars for ourselves and others into every spectrum of life. It's time to transform your world into something blissful and profoundly worthwhile.

11

*Practice all around fulfillment
by staying in your lane.*

Life is an intricate mix of the good, the bad, and the ugly. However, you choose the nature of meaning in your life. If you choose to accept the circumstances of your life as they are, you can push towards all around fulfillment. If you decide to spend time wishing you were more like someone else, life will never reveal its true beauty. The reality of this strategy might seem easy, but it's challenging in practice. When we hold too much negative energy, due to past regrets or disappointments, we're always waiting around for something to change—for our kids to grow up, or to receive a promotion, take a vacation, or even retire.

Instead, choose to connect and engage with life. Your existence will otherwise wither away, and the unfulfilling forces at play will devalue your self-image, until at last you're no better than a robot, simply around to run basic functions and pass the time. In the words of Carl Jung, **"We cannot change anything until we accept it, condemnation does not liberate, it oppresses."** You must understand that you cannot defeat certain forces in life and end up happy. To love your life, try accepting it unconditionally, thereby letting go of everything you cannot control.

We think that happiness fills the void, making our struggles and difficulties magically evaporate. If that were so, why do these struggles still plague us? The reality is that until we understand the true essence of our challenges, happiness will continue to elude us. Pain is there to remind us that we are not in control. You must learn to stay within your lane. This means that you have no business trying to control or poke your head into other people's affairs. Life itself is more significant than you; it will have its way every time. In the armory of life, there's a large box of tricks born from decades of experience—compared to your humble few years of existence. If you want to love life, you must dance with it in harmony.

Many times, our thinking process stops us from achieving such harmony. We feel that achieving a bank account full of money, a luxury home, or a fancy car is an expression of happiness; however, while these things are valuable on their own, they are meaningless when it comes to true happiness. This is because learning to love your life begins from within; it has no business with exteriors. According to John Campbell, **"we must let go of the life we planned and instead accept that which is waiting for us."**

The nature of your interactions depends on the meanings you endow them with. Your actions are the critical factor in defining the expressions and emotions you feel, and this determines your quality of life. Therefore, when you distort life's meanings, viewing events through fractured glass, that's how life will look to you. You must check if your thought patterns are helping or causing harm. It's crucial that you understand how perception informs experience. When we see something as negative, we respond to it in that light, creating emotions which reinforce that version of reality.

Sometimes in life, people do things that hurt us considerably. It seems more natural to live within distorted perceptions, because if we open ourselves up, we might get hurt again. Living like that robs you of any opportunity to fall in love with life, but if you let go of that anger, releasing your judgments and self-hate, you allow yourself heal. To otherwise keep harboring the same fears, pains, and emotions means that you never detached from the event—you're letting it continue to hurt you, and such is a toxic contamination of your future.

You must reframe the way you see the future, because although you cannot control people's actions or feelings, you can control your own response. You can derive meaning from positive or negative details, but you cannot derive happiness from pain. You can either be the ambassador or the victim, whichever you choose. It may not be easy, but it's possible. If you let go of the past and embrace your wholesome future, happiness can be yours.

ACTION STEPS!

STEP 1 Acknowledge that you've been pretending too long— you're ready to create a new future. Denying reality does not make it go away, but you have the power to change and create the future. Accept that it's okay to have these challenges right now. Give yourself the opportunity to work towards your dreams.

STEP 2 Acknowledge what you've done in the past—the roles you've played, whether good or bad, using a spectator's point of view. Ask yourself what can be done to remedy these situations. Find a pen and write down the solution. Once you know how to deal with it, take the necessary steps.

STEP 3 So you've made a lot of mistakes—maybe you did some really terrible things—but whatever. It's not about who you were, it's about who you're becoming. Simply admit that you've made mistakes and decide to move forward. Begin by writing down your failures and then proceed to strike them out. Next, seek out your strengths, write them down and concentrate hard on their reality. You can wait around until you get everything you need, or you can realize that it's not about getting things—it's about finding the tools to care for yourself.

STEP 4 Realize that in working towards a brighter future, you won't always get things right, but don't beat yourself up about it or try to rewrite history. History is already too good at rewriting itself. Own up to the consequences and push forever forwards. Love yourself through the good and the bad.

STEP 5 It's okay that you have fears, failures, and insecurities; billions of people do, but it's all about your choices. Will you dwell in fear or forge forwards into life? Take a look in the mirror, finding your strengths and focusing on them. Count your blessings and find the tools to improve yourself from within.

STEP 6 Don't get caught up thinking about how things *should* be; simply work on what is possible now. Ignore society's recipes for happiness. Find a journal and write down the desires no one else understands; validate them as true for yourself and commit to chasing them. Patience is a challenging virtue to learn, but when you accept things as they are, you amplify patience. With patience hard at work, various external factors can blend together and produce the profound reward of **peace**. When we're patient, we strengthen in resolve, and our desires manifest in time. More than anything, we learn patience through acceptance.

Appreciate the sacredness of the moment.

Becoming detached from the present moment makes it very difficult to appreciate your life. When did you last express gratitude for the beauty surrounding you? When did you last express gratitude for the passionate people all across the world? When was the last time you gave thanks to God—for the simple gift of life, for your friends and family, and all the valuable lessons life has waiting for you. When was the last time you displayed appreciation for all that is precious and rare? Take a good look in your bedroom mirror and appreciate the fire in your eyes.

Break away from life's busy schedule and take a moment to feel God running through you. Permit yourself to relax, let go of all that stress, fear, anxiety, and doubt, trusting that life will reveal the solution. I'd say that we stress ourselves out more than we enjoy life. We worry about all kinds of things, both big and small, bad and good, instead of focusing on the beauty and loveliness of our lives. We feel more at ease talking about our challenges, the wrongs of the past or mistakes of the present, and everything we see going wrong in the future.

We have lost the character we had as kids. Enjoying life, being at complete peace with where we're at right now, no longer comes easy. Instead, we constantly try to acquire more things and blossom into greater beings, always feeling like there's something we haven't done. We waste our vital life forces chasing after moreish dreams, until we lose touch with who we are. We have forgotten the beautiful reasons behind our existence; we are no longer Human Beings but Human Doings. We've become robots, operating in the name of excess.

It's time you changed that perception. Learn to embrace what makes you unique, beautiful, and human. You're not a machine nor a robot; you're a human being with a heart, not an engine. You have emotions and feelings designed to love, appreciate, and enjoy your life. Stop moving around like a crazy person and trying to do so much. Stop running so fast, because the monster lives inside your head. Slow down and feel the steady flow of your pulse, the stores of energy and wisdom within your body. Feel the life in your life! No more autopilot, get into the driver's seat and take control. Express gratitude for everything life has offered up until this moment and work on appreciating the little things most of all.

Always remember, life is a journey with a final destination, so enjoy each day as if it's your last. Love the "little" you have right now, because it makes up big parts of who you are. Your life is happening today. There's no pause button, so stop waiting around for things to change. Treasure each moment and appreciate the power of now.

Gratitude causes joy to surge through your life. When you adopt an attitude of appreciation, you see the world differently. You understand how hardship is balanced out by blessings. You become more sensitive to the exceptional variety of detail in the world, being grateful for every new day, every fresh breath, for one's health and family, for Mother Nature and all her wild elements— her rains and fogs and winds and thunderstorms forever crackling with light.

When you're not grateful enough for the present moment and all the miraculous forces it includes, happiness remains a mirage. You'll never be at peace. Always there will be moments of desiring for more, but if you're after a miracle, learning to embrace the present is a good place to start.

ACTION STEPS!

STEP 1 When you write things down, you remember them anew; therefore, take five minutes every morning to write down the beautiful blessings of the present moment. You'll be surprised by the enormity of magic in your life. Sometimes, yesterday's challenges roll over and try to obscure your blessings—push them away and focus on what you have. You'll be filled by energy and contentment, harnessing the zeal to delve into your day.

STEP 2 Use sticky notes to remember what makes you grateful. These can be addressed to other people as well. They concern things that you should be thankful about.

Review them regularly and notice how wonderfully blessed you are.

STEP 3 Practice gratitude in many settings, as explained in earlier chapters. Your practice of gratitude could begin at meal times. Talk about the best parts of your day. Show your kids how grateful you are for the present moment, with all its little gifts and eccentricities. Concentrate not on material things but moments and people.

STEP 4 Start a daily gratitude journal. List out the things you're grateful for every day. For instance, I'm thankful for being able to take a shower, brush my teeth, start the car, say *hi* to my neighbors, and get dressed on my own. What are you grateful for? List everything out and be grateful for what you have.

STEP 5 Obviously, it's easier to appreciate the big stuff. Noticing the small stuff takes more attention, but sometimes the small stuff is the important stuff. Learn to appreciate the smell of chocolate chips, that crisp new shirt, a warm cup of tea, or that big ball of fire in the sky. Keep listing out the little things, remembering the moments and meanings attached to them.

STEP 6 After overcoming a challenge, we often feel more gratitude. We dwell less in negative moments and feel empowered by what we've overcome. When you go to bed, leave your mind in a positive place. Think about what you achieved during the day, instead of where you fell short, and let the wonder of those feelings encompass you.

STEP 7 Make it a habit to live in the present. Forget living in the past or trying to override the future. Automatically switch your default setting to appreciating the present.

Flood your mind with blessings and watch as God becomes transparent. You are so much more—right here and now.

Keep fear and worry away from tomorrow.

When you fear tomorrow, you forget that yesterday was dangerous too. Let go of your hold on yesterday and embrace today with contentment. While many of us seek joy and happiness, we won't all attain these things. Nonetheless, this inner desire exists inside us all. The problem we face in finding joy often emanates from holding onto things too tightly. We're too serious about extinguishing threats to our happiness, and this brings us despair. If you wish to find fulfillment, you must first detach from the outcome.

Start by recognizing your true self, and enjoy the security of being you! By detaching from desire, you can approach decisions, actions, and relationships with objectivity. When you attain full detachment, you become fully involved in achieving your goals. You amass the capacity to step out of character, letting go of your dreams and plans, and thereby making room to reflect. In the words of Ron W. Rathbun, '**True detachment from life is not being disconnected from life, but attaining absolute freedom to explore the living.**" But how do you become detached, and what's the difference between this and wanting?

To begin with, when you're totally detached, you feel disconnected from the following feelings: fear, anxiety, jealousy, hopelessness, sadness, pride, vanity, disconnection. All of these emotions arise from being too attached—whether it's to money, social status, jobs, or relationships. Let's say you want to take an outrageous workshop that seems entirely over-budget; if you're too attached to the impossibility, financial anxiety will consume you, but if you take a moment to be grateful, you might think, *If the money shows up, I'll take the course. If it doesn't, no biggie; I can do it some other time.* In being too attached, you give external forces the power to control you. You might tell yourself that without "person x" you'd be helpless and unfulfilled, but probably this isn't true.

Detachment transforms desire into a choice, and ironically, this keeps us from desiring with fear and worry. When you relax about the outcome through detachment, your passion becomes a choice—we call this free will. What you wished *would be* becomes *what is*, dissolving all doubt, hatred, jealousy, and fear, essentially lessening the load on your heart. Your choice becomes your will, thereby liberating you in the process.

When overly attached, we tend to let external forces define us, ascribing our entire personhood to one entity. However, without that entity, you're still you—realize this and begin moving towards fulfillment. Never confuse detachment with quitting, because detachment does not mean neglecting your goals. Instead it means becoming calm enough to confront the challenges of the present moment. When we overthink, worry, or become too attached, we often pick desperate solutions for our problems. Most of these don't help; sometimes they even make things worse.

When you're too attached to outcomes, you remain in a state of resistance: your mind fills with negative energy—but when you detach from the problem, there's no resistance. Panic becomes peace, and peace takes the stable form of certainty. When you attain this state, life flows naturally in all directions—your desires become choices, which create your reality. In this state, you maximize your thought-power and align with your preferences, becoming a ball of attraction for what you desire. Enjoy this process, for it leads towards actualizing your dreams. When you become detached, life turns into the best game of your life.

Personally, when I have a problem I can't solve, I become nervous and even lose track of my surroundings. Slowly, this little problem magnifies itself, destroying my state of mind. This is a common problem when it comes to overthinking. We become consumed by the thought process, until our ability to function and care for those around us is destroyed. However, when you detach from the problem, you make room for new solutions.

ACTION STEPS!

STEP 1 Take a step back and consider the thoughts that enter your mind on a daily basis. What does reality consist of for you? Let your mind drift to the past and reflect on earlier events, watching what happens when situations threaten to overwhelm you. Also, notice the effect that these challenges have on your body, with all their stress and depressive feelings. Take note of behavioral patterns that don't seem to work and make small changes. By understanding these patterns, you find new strategies for changing them.

STEP 2   In such situations, remember to think about what happens to your ego. For instance, your ego might convince you that you didn't get the job because you're not smart enough; by extension, you've ruined your career. In reality, that job wasn't yours in the first place. There was no gain or loss; you're making up that situation in your mind. Your future potential remains intact, if only you'd accept it.

STEP 3   Furthermore, sometimes opening your mind to life's uncertainties triggers a natural state of detachment. According to Deepak Chopra, "when you seek the security of your exterior, you're only letting yourself into an endless chase that brings about nothing." However, by relinquishing your attachment to the illusion of security, thereby latching onto the unknown, you step beyond the realm of challenge and enter the kingdom of endless possibilities. It's here that you find abundance, fulfillment, and pure happiness.

STEP 4   When faced with challenges that threaten to overwhelm you, try meditating. Meditation releases your mind from these thought patterns. Engage in daily reflection on God's promises. Upon detaching from your hardships, you'll learn to identify infallible solutions.

STEP 5   Don't beat yourself up over your problems. When you get frustrated or fall into old habits, detach yourself from negativity and focus on change. Detachment allows ideals to become reality, occupying every nook and crevice of your physical world. When you let yourself get attached, it breeds panic and disempowerment, but on the other side of this experience is peace of mind and self-certainty. When you realize that your outside world is a reflection of your inner world, detachment becomes as natural and effortless as air.

14

Being carefree creates clarity in all situations.

In Chapters 4 and 9, we discussed being lighthearted, but now we must integrate this habit into our lives. In the past, I was often so rigid that I found playful or cheerful people to be false or inauthentic. I said to myself, without fully understanding, *How can they be so carefree, when all I do is worry?* I always felt that being carefree was irresponsible, but as I began to undergo this training, I realized that being carefree or content did not mean letting go of my dreams or being irresponsible—it meant being able to enjoy life in the moment, without worrying too much about what came next.

When playful, we connect with our true selves. Deep down, we're all just little kids whose bodies have grown up, but it's time to re-engage the child within you. Eventually, I came to understand why some people seemed so playful, joyful, and carefree: they'd already achieved a lot of success in their lives. By being light-hearted, we don't turn away from our goals and responsibilities, but we do learn to take deeper breaths. Through lightheartedness, I built a deeper connection with my family, friends, and future acquaintances. I adopted the effortless and fashionable lifestyle trend of celebrating my dreams and aspirations with contagious laughter, improving my relationships with a steady flow of positive energy, warmth, and tender connection.

I believe that lightheartedness makes it easier to resolve conflicting situations, by way of lessening the emotional load. Stress and tension are minimized within ourselves, making this state easier to achieve. We are prepared for whatever life throws at us. The more we laugh and remain open to merriment, the more that warm emotions begin coursing through our bodies, elevating our mood to the sky. Lightheartedness brings greater flexibility and openmindedness to challenging situations, freeing up alternative ways of solving problems. When we're tense or too serious, it's tricky to think outside our feelings and find the right answers. Lightheartedness helps uncover creative solutions for our problems. In the previous sections, you've seen the benefits of being lighthearted; now we'll learn habits to use lightheartedness as a catalyst for transforming your life.

ACTION STEPS!

STEP 1   For one thing, practice the habit of smiling. When you smile often, you become more attractive, likable, and approachable. Even when the pain and confusion of life seems to overwhelm us, smiling can lighten your emotional state. People gravitate towards you when you smile. According to research, telephone listeners can hear if someone is smiling, even without seeing them. Smiling literally effects our tone of voice, making other people feel more comfortable talking to us. When we practice smiling, we begin to find the right solutions. As well, further research shows that when we smile, our brain cools down, and when we frown, it heats up. It's like we have central air conditioning—so take advantage of your inner coolants and start beaming at the world.

STEP 2   Learn to laugh at all times, even if everything is falling apart—if your life is literally falling apart, try to laugh at that too. Laugh at your sheer dumb luck and how little you can do about it! Surrender to the power of the universe and feel its inscrutable beauty confound you. Laughter increases alertness, creativity, and productivity, while also decreasing muscle tension, so even when the light at the end of the tunnel seems ridiculously far away *(like, who would ever make such a long tunnel anyways)*, be thankful that you can laugh.

STEP 3   Listen to your heart to understand when feelings of hurt or anger are stuck inside you. These feelings might not come with solutions for managing the world, but they'll teach you about yourself. Becoming aware of your feelings is not about overwhelming yourself with emotions though. Rather, it's about finding better strategies for managing your responses to them. Write down these feelings and include how they made you behave. Now think about strategies you might use in these challenging moments, ones that have worked for you in the past. Upon finding these sunny spots in your behavior, use the attached strategies to resolve similar situations in your life. In starting with our successes, we gain the confidence to resolve our shortcomings, preparing ourselves to peacefully address moments that otherwise might be ruined by negative emotions.

STEP 4 Ok, so life is blowing its share of problems your way—decide then and there to just let go. This requires accepting the existence of your problems and realizing that they cannot take you over. Do not take them too seriously. As a human, you're capable of the impossible, except when you let your negative energy overflow. Step into light-heartedness by detaching from needing total power over your life. Then when life blows a stormy weather system your way, you'll be prepared to dance in the rain.

STEP 5 Take time—lots of it—to reconvene and regroup alone. Know what you love and integrate it physically, emotionally, mentally, socially, creatively, and spiritually. Use this newfound knowledge to have a lighthearted approach towards your everyday life. The more you practice these habits, the more you'll find solace and belief in your power, bravely facing whatever challenges come your way.

*Access your life from
a wholesome dimension.*

For most people, weekdays include a chain of repetitive activities: wake-up, check phone/computer, take a shower, drink coffee, drive in morning traffic, work, work, work, drive in evening traffic, have screen time, sleep (hard), toss, turn, **repeat**. For me though, day-times look more like this: 5am workout, meditation, meal prep, breakfast with my family, work, work, work, spend time with my family, and finally hit the hay—no TV, no news, no screen time.

A lot of people say their jobs are too hectic, but that's not the point. Your career is about having a specific role or purpose. However, if you cannot first amend your everyday routines, getting inspired to change your life will be tough. Faced with changing routines, it sometimes feels easier to stick to what's familiar—changing requires effort, and always this feels daunting. *Where do I start? How does one add fun and inspiration to their life, anyways?*

Freedom is not about having unlimited money and zero work responsibilities. A lot of people lose sense of this. The liberty I'm talking about is different; it's about doing anything you want, any time you want, and always working with purpose. You'll never be free doing someone else's bidding, so when it comes to someone else's dream, climbing the corporate ladder might be less satisfying than expected. Freedom is more about pursuing what is most important to you; it's about taking advantage of every opportunity and fully experiencing the world's beauty. Freedom is not about the open highway, but finding the road map to drive towards your goals.

ACTION STEPS!

STEP 1 Take time to express your whole self. Many times we get stuck in appearances or routines, forgetting the effort it took to get there. Take time to let every aspect of yourself shine through, in business, life, and family, letting the world see who you truly are. We discussed self-love in the first section of this book, but sometimes self-love must be proactive. Start by taking an inventory of your life, noticing how much there is to cherish and appreciate.

STEP 2 Tons of people work jobs that they don't really like, usually for the money. When we spend time doing things we don't enjoy, we wither away. This affects us slowly but in more ways than we can imagine, so take your time to answer these questions: Are you working your dream job? Do someone else's dreams propel you forward? What do you really want, and when do you want it?

STEP 3 Take time to create a genuine opportunity for yourself. This might mean stepping away from your home and family for a moment. Think about your interests, passions, and professional relationships. This productive reflection lets you redefine your life. However, please don't focus on negative thoughts—it's simply not worth it. We're trying to create a new you, and while a different career might mean less money, it comes with greater peace of mind. Be patient with this process, giving yourself space to grow.

STEP 4 Be open to new directions and wisdom, as they could guide you towards happiness. Perhaps find a life coach or engage with new skills. You might even choose to explore YouTube and subscribe to an online course. The bottom line is that you must get involved in something new, thereby opening fresh pathways and possibilities in your life.

STEP 5 When we reach the end of our lives, we don't remember all the material things we've acquired, but we might remember our most profound experiences. Remember to do everything you desire in life, but don't be hasty. Wait for the right time, gaining new experiences as you need them. All in all, try to be happy.

STEP 6 Take a good look at the children in your life; they're your best role models when it comes to this step. Let them remind you how to live with a sense of playfulness. If you have an old hobby you want to take up again, go for it. It's time to play, but not just in your free time—now we must learn to incorporate play into every aspect of our lives.

STEP 7　Learn to take life one step at a time and beware of doing everything at once. Redefining your life is an obvious challenge: your family might not get it, your friends might not understand, and all of this makes doubting yourself easy. Nonetheless, hold onto the purity of your intentions. You want to enjoy and be fulfilled by your life, and this starts with doing what you love.

Anne's Story

Anne is a client and friend of mine. Athough she seemed to have it all, Anne felt that something was missing from her life. She had a high-powered career and a well-connected husband. They had three lovely kids, who did well in school and got along with their peers. Their tight-knit family seemed happy, healthy, and financially secure; they even took family vacations from time to time.

However, Anna was struggling, and it bothered her a whole lot. She said her job was all-consuming, but her co-workers depended heavily on her expertise. She worried that things would fall apart if she wasn't around all the time. She wanted to be home with her family earlier and feel more connected to her kids. Her pillars were indeed out of balance.

After many coaching lessons together, she discovered that her unhealthy work habits had started with her parents, who valued work over everything else. They'd created work environments that encompassed their entire lives. Anne needed to reprogram her perspectives on success and self-worth, before seeing that progress was defined by much more than material things.

Anne set new boundaries at work and started delegating tasks to other employees, giving everyone a chance to become better employees. She created time for her family and hobbies. As she reconnected with her loved ones' honest desires, positive changes began to take effect in her life. She began to live fully and wholesomely, full of fond memories and moments blessed with potential.

Summary

Let us use a life-changing event: You wish to open a new business, but somehow there's no money to push it through. Also, it would take much more than a mortgage to get it together. The First Pillar is Acceptance: accept that presently you do not have the funds to push your business into reality. Don't compare yourself to Mr. A or Mrs. B, who have the resources to emerge with start-up companies at any time. Be satisfied with your progress and identify strategies to make yourself even happier.

The Second Pillar is Appreciation. If you cannot foot those bills right now, no problem—it does not change who you are. Appreciate your capacity to dream. In so many people, the capacity to dream has been destroyed, and their passions are mysteries to them. There are people on their deathbeds who've only just realized their true purpose, without any time left to work towards it. You have the time and power to turn your purpose into a lifestyle. You have the imagination to conceive of your future, the mind to construct it, and the time to turn it into reality.

The Third Pillar is Desire: focus on your passions but detach from the results. Worry, jealousy, and envy threaten to cloud your mind. Your friends and family might try to convince you to abandon your dreams; respect their opinions, but don't internalize their feelings. Keep an objective view of your desires and watch as solutions take form.

The Fourth Pillar is Lightheartedness. Let go of all that seriousness and learn to take things as they come. Of course, try taking little steps towards your goals, but don't force them into being. Assume a playful stance and have a sense of humor—most likely, the universe will come out to play.

The Fifth Pillar is Freedom of Self-Expression. Perhaps you dream of being independent, but if you let negative emotions cloud your thinking, obsessing over the present impossibility of this desire, you'll only exchange physical dependence for mental slavery. Instead, learn to express yourself in difficult moments; expression comes from within and belongs entirely to you. In the words of George Bernard Shaw, "We don't stop playing because we grow old; we grow old because we stop playing."

CONCLUSION

In the process of redefining your pillars of love, for self, life, and others, you've recognized who you are and uncovered your true goals. Now it's time to take action. So far you've focused on making proactive changes in specific areas of life, using love as the first stepping stone. Now we'll focus on allowing love to help you surmount obstacles. Love can also provide insight into the external and internal barriers that keep you from your higher purpose. You may have noticed that the wealthiest rewards come from having a steady flow of love in our lives.

There's little that cannot be cured by love. If you don't feel adequately loved, give love out abundantly. If you feel like the world does not love you enough, love yourself more. If you receive toxic love, do not respond with the same energy. No one has the power to stop the flow of love within you, unless you step aside and let them. Love should not exist with conditions. Love means striving to be compassionate, understanding, and tolerant in all facets of life. If people threaten to harm you, simply ensure that your actions are rooted in the five pillars—let them nourish your spirit endlessly.

WORKS CITED

Baumeister, Roy, and John Tierney. *Willpower: Rediscovering the Greatest Human Strength.* Penguin Random House, 2012.

Bold, Scott. "How to Create More Freedom in Your Life Everyday." *FreedomFastLane*, 2 Sept. 2013, www.freedomfastlane.com/how-to-create-more-freedom-in-your-life-everyday/. Accessed Jan. 2019.

Braden, Gregg. *The Divine Matrix; Bridging Time, Space, Miracles, and Belief.* Hay House Inc., 1 Jan. 2008.

"The Story of the Taoist Farmer." *BrianTaylor*, 2 Feb. 2019, http://www.briantaylor.com/TaoistFarmerStory.html. Accessed Jan. 2019.

Burke, Fauzia. "11 Ways to Appreciate Your Life a Little More." *MindBodyGreen*, www.mindbodygreen.com/0-16408/11-ways-to-appreciate-your-life-a-little-more.html. Accessed Jan. 2019.

Chopra, Deepak. *The Seven Spiritual Laws of Success: A Practical Guide to the Fulfillment of Your Dreams.* Amber-Allen Publishing, 1994.

Croft, Harry. "How to Open Up and Reveal Yourself to Others." *HealthyPlace*, 17 Sept. 2017, www.healthyplace.com/relationships/healthy-relationships/how-to-open-up-and-reveal-yourself-to-others. Accessed Jan. 2019.

Csikszentmihalyi, Mihaly. *Flow: The Psychology of Optimal Experience.* Harper Perennial Modern Classics, 2007.

Daskal, Lolly. "How to Accept Yourself, Your Life, and Your Reality." *Inc*, 15 Feb. 2018, www.inc.com/lolly-daskal/how-to-accept-yourself-your-life-your-reality.html. Accessed Jan. 2019.

Davenport, Barrie. "Live a Fulfilling Life: 25 Essential Ingredients for Happiness." *LiveBoldandBloom*, https://liveboldandbloom.com/06/self-improvement/living-fulfilling-life. Accessed Jan. 2019.

"Story of the Five Pillars of a Balanced Life." *DutchNomadFamily,* 12 Aug. 2007, www.dutchnomadfamily.com/story-five-pillars-balanced-life/. Accessed Jan. 2019.

Ecaldre, Pearl Marie. "50 Best Quotes About Overcoming Relationship Problems." *InspiringTips,* https://inspiringtips.com/best-quotes-overcoming-relationship-problems. Accessed Jan. 2019.

Ehrlich, Noreen. "How the Five Pillars of Life Help You Achieve Balance and Achievement." *Defy&Hustle,* www.noreenehrlich.com/how-the-5-pillars-of-life-help-you-achieve-balance-and-fulfillment/. Accessed Jan. 2019.

Fahkry, Tony. "If You Want to be Happy, Accept Life as It Is and Let Go of What You Cannot Control." *Medium,* 27 Oct. 2017, www.medium.com/the-mission/if-you-want-to-be-happy-accept-life-as-it-is-and-let-go-of-what-you-cannot-control-466ac638a45b. Accessed Jan. 2019.

"How to Appreciate What You Have and Stop Comparing Yourself to Others." *HappifyDaily,* www.happify.com/hd/how-to-appreciate-what-you-have/. Accessed Jan. 2019.

Hara, Carmen. "5 Pillars of a Joyful Life." *HuffPost,* 24 Jan. 2019, www.huffpost.com/entry/5-pillars-of-a-joyful-life_b_6186390. Accessed Jan. 2019.

Heitler, Susan. "How to Express Feelings…and How Not to." *PsychologyToday,* 23 May 2013, www.psychologytoday.com/us/blog/resolution-not-conflict/201305/how-express-feelings-and-how-not. Accessed Jan. 2019.

Hill, Napoleon. *Think and Grow Rich: Unabridged Text of the First Edition.* Lightning Source Inc., 2013.

Kotsos, Tania. "The Secret to Effortless Detachment." *MindYourReality,* www.mind-your-reality.com/detachment.html. Accessed Jan. 2019.

Lama, Dalai, Desmond Tutu, and Carlton Abrams. *The Book of Joy: Lasting Happiness in a Changing World.* Penguin Random House, 2016.

Lantz, Gregory L. "Redefining Your Purpose." *Psychology Today,* 23 Nov. 2013, www.psychologytoday.com/us/blog/hope-relationships/201311/ redefining-your-purpose. Accessed Jan. 2019.

"The Serenity Prayer." *LordsPrayersWords,* www.lords-prayer-words.com/ famous_prayers/god_grant_me_the_serenity.html. Accessed Jan. 2019.

"12 Most Important Ways to Let People Know They Matter." *AngelaMaiers,* May 2018, https://www.angelamaiers.com/blog/12-most-important-ways-to-let-people-know-they-matter.html. Accessed Jan. 2019.

Neuroskeptic. "The 70,000 thoughts per day myth?" DiscoverMagazine, 9 May 2012, http://blogs.discovermagazine.com/neuroskeptic/ 2012/05/09/the-70000-thoughts-per-day-myth/#.XBu0M1VKhdg. Accessed Jan. 2019.

Ritter, Al. *The 100/0 Principle: The Secret of Great Relationships.* Simple Truths, 2010.

Rosenblatt, Caroline. "Magic Touch: Six Things You Can Do to Connect in a Disconnected World." *Forbes,* 18 Jan. 2011, www.forbes.com/sites/ carolynrosenblatt/2011/01/18/magic-touch-six-things-you-can-do-to-connect-in-a-disconnected-world/#49cd6e0451af. Accessed Jan. 2019

Saviuc, Luminita D. "Appreciation: The Key to a Happy Life." *PurposeFairy*, 3 Sept. 2014, www.purposefairy.com/73664/appreciation-the-key-to-a-happy-life/. Accessed Jan. 2019.

Sellar, Stacey Yates. "The 5 Pillars of Happiness." *Medium*, 11 May 2017, www.medium.com/@happierbytheminute/the-5-pillars-of-happiness-c752648037db. Accessed Jan. 2019.

Stillman, Jessica. "How to Make Someone Feel Like the Most Important Person in the World: 5 Tips." *Inc,* 7 Sept.2017, www.inc.com/jessica-stillman/how-to-make-someone-feel-like-the-most-important-person-in-the-world-5-tips.html. Accessed Jan. 2019.

Talbot, Betsy & Warren. "10 Ways to Add More Freedom to Your Life." *AnUnclutteredLife,* Feb. 2016, https://player.fm/series/an-uncluttered -life/aul-144-10-ways-to-add-more-freedom-into-your-life. Accessed Jan. 2019.

Thomas, Camille. "12 Ways to Exercise and Express Your Personal Freedom." *Medium*, 26 Apr. 2018, www.medium.com/@dili- gentcopy/12-ways-to-exercise-and-express-your-personal-free- dom-13ad5168d12a. Accessed Jan. 2019.

Williamson, Marianne. "Our Deepest Fear." *HabitsforWellBeing,* https:// www.habitsforwellbeing.com/our-deepest-fear/. Accessed Jan. 2019.

Zing, Zue. "Five Pillars You Can Build That Will Enhance the Quality of Your Life." *TheAscent,* 6 Oct. 2017, www.theascent.pub/5-pillars-you- can-build-that-will-enhance-the-quality-of-your-life-4ae55c1b0f09. Accessed Jan. 2019.